From Angels to Hellcats

LEGENDARY TEXAS WOMEN, 1836 TO 1880

DON BLEVINS

Mountain Press Publishing Company
Missoula, Montana
2001

Library of Congress Cataloging-in-Publication Data

Blevins, Don, 1933–
    From angels to hellcats: legendary Texas women,
    1836 to 1880 / Don Blevins.
        p. cm.
    ISBN 0-87842-443-1 (alk. paper)
        1. Women pioneers—Texas—Biography.
    2. Frontier and pioneer life—Texas. 3. Texas—
    Biography. 4. Texas—History—Republic,
    1836–1846—Biography. 5. Texas—History—
    1846–1950—Biography. I. Title.

F390 .B67 2001
976.4—dc21
                                        2001044745

PRINTED IN THE UNITED STATES OF AMERICA

Mountain Press Publishing Company
P.O. Box 2399, Missoula, MT 59806
406-728-1900

To my wife, Esther, and the four Ds:
David, Donna, Dennis, and Debbie

And to the fascinating story of Texas's past

Contents

Acknowledgments

Many people and agencies go into any study of history. I especially appreciate the staff of the Daughters of the Republic of Texas Library at the Alamo in San Antonio, particularly Martha Utterback and Cathy Herpich. Accolades also to assistance rendered by the expert staffs at the Center for American History on the University of Texas campus and the Texas State Library and Archives, both in Austin. Special thanks to John Anderson.

The assistance of Hugh and Tom Hornsby in gathering information on the Hornsby clan was invaluable. Maxine Reilly, director of the Refugio County Museum, came through with Sally Scull information when I thought all was lost.

And of course my gratitude to Gwen McKenna, editor, who helped turn this project into a presentable piece of work. Your expertise goes beyond all expectations.

There are many others whose help I could not have done without. Be assured, any slight is due to my weak memory retention, not lack of appreciation.

Introduction

The mystique of Texas, as much legend as fact, has been invoked and embellished many times over, in television, movies, books, and classrooms. The events—the fight for independence, the Alamo, the Goliad massacre—are all elements of the saga that is Texas history. But the events are only part of the story—it's the people who make history come alive. The Lone Star State has had its share of colorful people: Houston, Travis, Bowie, Crockett, wildcatters, cattle barons, outlaws, peace officers. Somewhere in the mix are women, little known (if known at all) but extraordinary. These women lived on the line between good and bad, right and wrong, dark and light.

No period in American history was more ripe for men and women to be themselves, decent or otherwise, than the mid- to late nineteenth century—the early decades of Texas growth. The territory went from a colony under Mexican aegis, to a land settled by Anglo Americans (most of whom professed little loyalty to anyone other than themselves), to a republic of independents, to a state. Throughout it all, Texas was as wild and woolly a frontier as any mining camp or mountain outpost in the West.

It is understandable that people living in this environment, practically free of legal and moral restraint, would lead lives unthinkable in the civilized Victorian society of the East. These women—who didn't hesitate to strap on a gun (and use it when necessary), or drink, gamble, steal, lie, curse, or spit, both on the ground and in the face of convention—would have been social outcasts elsewhere. But in Texas, they were admired, albeit at times begrudgingly. They earned then, and still earn, respect for their strength, courage, and perseverance—as do the women of Texas today.

The motto popular at the time, GTT (Gone to Texas), was certain to draw all forms of life to this new, wide-open territory. While Sam Houston, William Travis, and Stephen Long carved their place in Texas history and legend, there were also those who would not achieve the same fame—many of them women—but who nonetheless had a profound impact on the development of the state. Their personal epics have been hidden in the shadows of history. These women made their own trails, dared anyone to stop them, and lived lives they themselves shaped.

This book contains the stories of eight such women. While some of them offer a touch of speculation or hearsay, they are true stories. One of these women witnessed the horror of the Alamo and lived to tell about it. Another herded horses, defied Northern blockades during the Civil War, and admitted shooting her husband. Still another, an eighteen-year-old Mexican woman, came to the rescue of the Americans, her sworn enemy, during the Texas Revolution. Yet these women are only representative of many others who blazed similar trails.

These eight women lived in the wildest times this country ever experienced, times that will never again exist, a fact for which we should be grateful. While history may judge them angels or devils, in the end it matters little. They were, above all, people, plain and simple, making their way in a turbulent world.

I wonder how many of us could have survived it so well?

Don Blevins
San Marcos, Texas

Author note: In this book I have used the term "Texian" to describe Anglo-Texas residents before the revolution, in accordance with T. R. Fehrenbach's *Lone Star* and other Texas histories.

Susanna Dickinson

ALAMO SURVIVOR

The epic 1960 John Wayne film *The Alamo* contained numerous historical errors, as anyone familiar with Texas history can recognize. The legendary film embellished an event that needed no embellishment. The drama that was the Alamo stands alone in the annals of American history as an example of the human struggle for independence and the lengths to which men will go to attain it.

Some of the inaccuracies in the film surround the person of Susanna Dickinson, the only adult Anglo to survive the Alamo tragedy. In the closing scene of the movie, Susanna is shown leaving the remains of the fortress, her daughter astride a mule with Susanna alongside. A young black boy holds the reins of the animal. The "Ballad of the Alamo," sung so plaintively by the late Marty Robbins, comes hauntingly through as the trio walks defiantly in front of General Santa Anna and the remainder of his overpowering army. The troops stand silently, supposedly in respect, with the Mexican general going so far as to doff his Napoleonic headgear, ostensibly in honor of the gallant Texians who had just been annihilated by his troops.

Never let it be said that Hollywood lets the facts interfere with a good story.

To begin with, Susanna would have been unable to walk alongside the mule because she had earlier been shot in the leg, either accidently or on purpose, by a Mexican soldier. The young girl portraying her daughter, Angelina, appeared to be three or four years old, while the Angelina of 1836 was only fifteen months of age. The young black boy, in historical truth, was an adult, the servant of either Santa Anna or James Bowie —opinions differ.

Another discrepancy between the movie and fact is that Susanna did not march off into the sunset from the smoldering remains of the Alamo. She had been treated for her leg wound at a private home, and it was there that Santa Anna visited her. She left San Antonio from that house, not from the mission.

But the biggest absurdity involves Santa Anna. The general, who was president of Mexico at the time, would never have given the slightest sign of respect to the brave Americans behind the mission's crumbling walls. In truth, Santa Anna despised gringos and had vowed to leave Texas soil running with the blood of any and all Anglos—and Mexicans—who took up arms against the central government in Mexico City. That he would have removed his hat to his vile enemy is poppycock.

The Alamo did portray some of the facts of that fateful day in March 1836 correctly. Susanna Dickinson was the widow of artillery captain Almeron Dickinson, who, along with 188 comrades, had died in the battle. Susanna and her fifteen-month old daughter, Angelina, were the only Anglos to leave the mission alive. There the movie ends. A week after the fall of the Alamo, after Susanna had delivered the shocking news to General Sam Houston, she and her daughter faded from view. Her full story has seldom been told.

Susanna Dickinson
—Courtesy Texas State Library and Archives Commission

3

Susanna's story begins in the backwoods of west Tennessee, in Hardeman County, near Memphis. Born of country stock in 1814, Susanna Wilkerson could neither read nor write. Women were taught at home in the basics of cooking, keeping house, and caring for their families. It was considered a waste of time and money to send them to school. For this reason alone, Susanna could never establish herself in historical annals. She could not leave written testimony of where she had been and what she had seen. Only by secondhand reports through newspapers and family stories could her story be told.

A hint of the kind of life that lay ahead for Susanna occurred when she met her future husband. Almeron Dickinson was born in Pennsylvania and migrated to Tennessee. He met Susanna, who was only fifteen years old, soon after relocating to Hardeman County and attempted to court her. She rejected his advances, for reasons unknown, causing the young swain to look elsewhere. The object of his rerouted affection was a friend of Susanna's, and when the more willing lady accepted Almeron's proposal, she asked Susanna to be one of the bridesmaids. The day before the wedding, Almeron rode up to the Wilkerson farm to get Susanna and take her to his fiancée's home, where she and the rest of the bridal party would remain until the big event.

No one knows exactly what happened as the two rode toward their destination, but something did. Susanna and Almeron stopped at the county court clerk's office in Bolivar, took out a marriage license, and were wed that day, May 24, 1829. The newlyweds, knowing they would be chastised for leaving the intended bride waiting at the church, decided it would be best to move to some other part of the state, far from family and friends.

There is little doubt that Almeron could have found work in his new neighborhood. He was adept in many fields: blacksmith, ferrier, sometimes veterinarian, dentist. Yet, two years later, he and Susanna turned up in Texas. It isn't known if their fortunes reversed in Tennessee, or if they were lured by the adventurous tales coming out of this enticing land to the west.

Marriage license of Almeron Dickinson and Susanna Wilkerson
—Courtesy Daughters of the Republic of Texas Library

The couple settled in the small community of Gonzales, about sixty miles from San Antonio. Almeron set up a blacksmith shop and the Dickinsons celebrated the birth of a daughter, Angelina Elizabeth, in December 1834. Almeron was ceded a Mexican land grant in nearby Caldwell County as part of the Green DeWitt Colony, but he and Susanna never settled there. The Texas rebellion against Mexico was gaining momentum, and Almeron volunteered his services to the Texians. He was appointed a lieutenant of artillery.

It was at Gonzales, the westernmost Anglo-American settlement, that the first shots in the Texas Revolution were fired. In 1828, the Mexican military had given settlers at Gonzales a small cannon to ward off Indians. Four years later, with relations between the Texas settlers and Mexico extremely tense, return of the cannon to the latter's control was requested. When the requisition was refused, Mexico sent a lieutenant and one hundred dragoons to retrieve the weapon. Word spread quickly among the Texas settlers of the events taking place at Gonzales, and soon the rebel force grew to more than one hundred and sixty. When the Mexican soldiers arrived demanding the cannon, the colonists mounted it on an ox cart, filled it with scrap iron as ammunition, and hauled it across the Guadalupe River to face the Mexican troops.

To show that their intention to keep the weapon was genuine, the Americans fired at the Mexicans, one of whom was killed. The renegades brandished a hand-made flag bearing a rough drawing of the cannon topped by a single star and the inscription "Come and Take It." The shot fired on October 2, 1835, resounded from the Sabine River to Mexico City. The fight for independence was on.

The small Mexican military unit sent to Gonzales did not return the colonists' fire; instead, it rode back to San Antonio at a fast gallop. The Texians, now at war, moved on to San Antonio, where the largest contingent of Mexican soldiers camped. General Martín Perfecto de Cos, brother-in-law of Santa Anna, was in charge of the troops there. The Texians forced him and his men to retreat to Mexico. Flushed with success, many Texians returned to their homes thinking the rebellion was over and that Mexico was defeated. Not everyone agreed, however. Colonel William Travis moved into the Alamo with a small force of men, Almeron Dickinson among them, and braced for battle.

Almeron missed his family, and in early February 1836 he sent Susanna a letter asking that she and the baby join him in San Antonio. Ramón Músquiz, once political chief of Bexar (which later became San Antonio), was an old Masonic acquaintance of Almeron and he invited the Dickinsons to stay at his hacienda. For the first few days, things stayed quiet. Then, on February 23, a lookout announced the arrival of a large Mexican army.

Travis ordered everyone into the Alamo. Almeron rode hard to the Músquiz hacienda and called for Susanna to jump on the back of his horse. Ironically, Almeron felt his family would be safer within the walls

The Alamo —Courtesy Daughters of the Republic of Texas Library

of the old mission. Hugging Angelina tightly to her, Susanna rode with her husband into the fortress.

Susanna and her young daughter were placed in a small room in the chapel. With her were fourteen other noncombatants, two black men (slaves of Travis and Bowie) and twelve Mexican women and children. During the fighting, in addition to checking and securing artillery, Almeron tended the injured throughout the fortress. Susanna helped him, often using parts of her clothing as bandages.

As the battle raged outside there was little to occupy Susanna's energies, and time passed slowly for many days. Little Angelina had even fewer diversions to hold her attention. In the few jovial moments the rebels were able to enjoy, Susanna bounced her daughter on her knee while Davy Crockett and John McGregor played musical duets, the former on the fiddle, the latter on his native country's bagpipes.

The defenders fought with heart, believing a relief column from General Houston was on its way. By March 3, however, Travis realized there would be no reinforcements. An incident then took place which has been disputed by many historians, but to which Susanna attested in more than one interview. Travis called his men into the courtyard and told them straightforwardly that there would be no relief. He then drew a line in the dirt with his saber. Facing the small force, he said that anyone who wanted to leave could do so by crossing the line. Only one Texian chose to do so, a man by the name of Louis "Moses" Rose. In many writings and television and movie productions—including the John Wayne film—the option was reversed: those who agreed to remain in the Alamo were invited to cross the line.

Understandably, Louis Rose (he acquired the moniker "Moses" because of his age—51—at the Alamo) has often been depicted as a coward. But he never had to face judgment for his desertion. After his escape from death, he went on to open a butcher shop in Nacogdoches, Texas. Interestingly, he served as a witness for claims made by heirs of Alamo defenders. He died in Logansport, Louisiana, in 1851. His gun is displayed at the Alamo museum.

For twelve days the ragged, untrained band of Texians successfully repelled Santa Anna's superior force of some two thousand soldiers. Then on Sunday, March 6, occupants of the mission, including Susanna, awakened to the strains of the "Deguello," a march dating back to the time of the Spanish-Moor conflict in Europe. Its meaning was clear—no mercy, no survivors.

At some point—the exact time is in dispute—Colonel Travis took a cat's-eye ring from his finger, threaded it onto a string, and tied it around Angelina's neck. The gesture was ominous in itself, because the ring had been given to Travis by his betrothed, Rebecca Cummings. The ring, at that moment, entered the roll call of history.

Intending to end the siege, Santa Anna threw his forces against the Texians. The first two assaults were beaten back. The third, however, made a breach in the fortress walls, and the Mexicans poured in. In hand-to-hand combat, each defender would eventually be slain.

During the final hours Susanna, still secreted in her room and protecting her child, watched as a sixteen-year-old boy stumbled into the room and tried to speak, his jaw shattered by gunfire. He held his bloody jaw with his hands in an attempt to make himself understood, but to no avail. He finally walked away.

There has been conjecture that Davy Crockett was not killed in the battle, but that he surrendered and was later shot on orders of Santa Anna. Susanna's story contradicted this: she stated that "Crockett ran into my room and fell on his knees beside me. He committed himself to God, went out and was soon killed."

Susanna saw the last defender, a man named Walker, killed in that room. Walker had raced in followed by

10

four Mexican soldiers. After they shot him they lifted him into the air on their bayonets like a sack of flour. Because of the darkness of the room and the thick cover of gun smoke, the soldiers overlooked Susanna and the others.

Less than an hour before Walker met his death, Almeron had rushed into the room and hugged his wife and child. He told Susanna about the breach, then exited, saber in hand. That was the last she saw of her husband. Soon, the only sound penetrating the thick walls of the mission was the slowly diminishing gunfire. The defenders had been beaten.

Susanna remained huddled in the room, along with the other women and children. A shadowy figure appeared in the doorway. "Is Mrs. Dickinson here?" a man asked, in broken English. The man was a Mexican colonel named Almonte, who had been educated in New Orleans. He called her name a second time, saying it was a matter of life and death. When Susanna approached Almonte, he informed her that she was to be taken to General Santa Anna.

Susanna and her daughter would be spared. Susanna knew that the person responsible for saving their lives was her friend Señora Músquiz. When the señora learned that Santa Anna was determined to sack the Alamo, she went to the general and personally pleaded for the lives of Susanna and Angelina. The Músquiz name was strong in south Texas, and Santa Anna agreed, adding that he had not declared war on women and children.

Susanna was led from what remained of the chapel. Once outside, she confronted for the first time the death and destruction the battle had wrought. Three pyres burned with the bodies of the fallen Texians. As Susanna stepped cautiously through the horror before her, she recognized Crockett's mutilated body, lying between the church and the two-story barracks building, his peculiar cap by his side.

Marching across the courtyard with her captors, Susanna suddenly felt a sharp pain in her right leg and stumbled to the ground. Almonte grabbed Angelina before her mother dropped her. Susanna had been shot, either intentionally or unintentionally, by a Mexican soldier. She was taken to the Músquiz hacienda, where her wound was treated.

Santa Anna soon appeared at the hacienda. The strongman was instantly captivated by the beautiful little girl in the wounded woman's arms. He asked Susanna to let him adopt the child, offering to take both of them to Mexico as his wards. There, they would enjoy comfort, wealth, and power, and Angelina would have the best of teachers.

The proposition outraged Susanna. This was the evil man responsible for the death of her husband, Angelina's father. She angrily and bitterly informed him she would rather see her daughter starve than be associated with a murderer. Not used to having his wishes refused, Santa Anna bristled. When Susanna requested to see her husband's body, she was informed that it had already been cast on a funeral pyre with the rest of his comrades.

Though the woman had insulted him, at the suggestion of his aides the general decided to release Susanna so she could carry the message of what had taken place at the Alamo. He penned a letter warning the Texians, Americans, and anyone else who resisted his orders what the penalty would be: death to the last rebel. Susanna was to carry the message to Sam Houston, who at the time was training a makeshift army in Gonzales.

Santa Anna assigned his black servant (or Bowie's servant), Ben, to accompany the woman and her child. The general also sent along some troops to escort the party, but they turned back only a mile or so from San Antonio, leery lest they meet up with some Texians.

A short time after leaving the mission, Susanna spied riders in the distance. She hid in some bushes with Angelina and Ben, afraid the horsemen might be Mexican soldiers. As the men came closer, Susanna realized they were Anglos. It was Deaf Smith, Houston's trusted scout, and his party, on their way to San Antonio to ascertain the status of the Alamo.

The scouts escorted the three travelers to Gonzales. When the eyewitness to the battle relayed what had taken place, her words sent both fear and rage through Houston and his men. But when Susanna added that a large Mexican contingent followed close behind, Houston knew he could not be rash. He would burn Gonzales and move the army eastward, away from the enemy. The Texians were in no condition to battle the strong Mexican army. They would bide their time, waiting for a ripe opportunity.

During her brief respite at Gonzales, a horrible realization hit Susanna: she was now a widow with a small child. Worse, she not only had to cope with her own loss and sorrows, she was also the bearer of the tragic news that would soon be delivered to many other widows.

Santa Anna never acknowledged the tremendous price his army paid for winning the militarily unimportant Alamo. The Texians lost 189 men; the Mexicans, about 600 wounded or killed.

For six weeks Houston kept moving his men east and south in what became known as the "Runaway Scrape," always staying a few miles ahead of Santa Anna. Then, on the afternoon of April 21, while the Mexicans enjoyed a siesta, some 910 Texians scurried across the plain of San Jacinto, on Buffalo Bayou (in today's Houston). Houston's forces took Santa Anna's roughly 1,400 men completely by surprise. This final battle in Texas's fight for independence lasted only eighteen minutes. The Texians soundly defeated Santa Anna's troops: 630 killed, 750 taken prisoner, including the general himself, who was captured the following day dressed in the uniform of an enlisted man. Only 9 Texians were killed and 30 wounded. Houston suffered a shattered ankle.

Following the Texian victory, Susanna and Angelina were escorted to what would soon become the city of Houston, where they faded into obscurity. The state of Texas did nothing to recognize Susanna's contributions for more than ninety years. The only traces of her life after the Alamo are recorded through a few newspaper interviews and limited family records.

The years in Houston were hard and heartbreaking ones for Susanna and her daughter. Susanna petitioned the state legislature to award five hundred dollars for support of Angelina, based on her father's service at the Alamo and prior. After some debate the legislature tabled the motion, fearing it would open the gate for others to demand compensation. Many officials felt the struggling new nation had more pressing financial problems.

The Texas legislature did pass a bill in December 1837 authorizing donation certificates in the amount of 640 acres to the heirs of Alamo defenders. Many beneficiaries delayed in applying for their grants, but when they did, they learned they needed proof that their relatives had been at the Alamo. They turned to Susanna, the only viable witness, who made several attestations regarding the presence or absence of certain individuals. In August 1839 Susanna received a grant of 640 acres, and in June 1855 she and Angelina received a bounty warranty for 1,920 more in Clay County.

In November 1837 Susanna began a string of ill-fated marriages. The first, following Almeron, was to a man named John Williams. Because his name is so common, it is difficult to trace through history. The marriage was short and stormy, and in her divorce petition Susanna charged Williams with abuse of both her and her daughter. The divorce was granted March 24, 1838.

Nine months later Susanna married Francis P. Herring, who made his living hauling water from

Beauchamps Spring to Houston, which was then relying on cisterns and wells for its water supply. Practically nothing more is known of Susanna's third husband. He died on September 15, 1843. To what degree the five-year marriage was happy or unhappy is impossible to tell.

On December 15, 1847, Susanna married Peter Bellows, age thirty-seven and, like her first husband, a native of Pennsylvania. By this time she was thirty-three and Angelina, thirteen. Bellows, sometimes listed as Bellis, made a fairly good living as a drayman, or freight hauler. This marriage lasted almost ten years, but it, too, was an unhappy union.

In 1857 Bellows petitioned for divorce on the grounds of desertion, beginning in the spring of 1854. He alleged that Susanna moved into a house of ill repute and, while there, committed adultery over a long period of time with a number of men. The case came to trial June 15, 1857. Bellows came with legal counsel; Susanna did not make an appearance. The court granted the divorce the same day.

Bellows might have been on solid ground with his claims. Susanna reputedly worked for a time in a boardinghouse that was, some claimed, a rather bawdy place known as the Mansion House. At one time the infamous and notorious Pamelia Mann, whose story is told in chapter five, owned the Mansion House. Under her proprietorship, the hotel was a brothel. Though it was sold when Mann died in 1840, it could well have continued as a "house of loose plays."

Meanwhile, Angelina grew up among the wild influences of the big city, becoming just as wild as her surroundings. Susanna prodded her into marrying a Montgomery County farmer by the name of John Maynard Griffith. The ceremony took place July 8, 1851, when Angelina was seventeen. While this was a mismatch from the beginning, the couple had children, who later would tell the story of the Alamo and their grandmother's role in it. The first child, a boy, was born in May 1853. Angelina named him Almeron Dickinson Griffith, for her father. Two years later, Angelina had a daughter, whom she named Susanna. The couple had their third and last child in 1857, a boy who was named Joseph, in honor of Susanna's new husband, Joseph William Hannig.

The marriage ended shortly after Angelina spent one night dancing with a number of men while her husband sat outside the dance hall caring for their young children. After the union was dissolved, the oldest boy went to live with his uncle, Joshua Griffith; the two younger children went with Susanna, their grandmother.

Free of all ties, both marital and parental, Angelina started drifting. In New Orleans she met and married a man named Holmes. She had another daughter, Sallie, and again dropped out of sight. Why and when that marriage ended and what became of Sallie is still a puzzle. Prior to the Civil War Angelina found her way to Galveston, where she met railroad man Jim Britton. There is no record that the two ever married, but she took his name. Britton enlisted in the Confederate army and departed for Tennessee. Angelina was left behind, but the ring William Travis had tied around her neck that final day in the Alamo accompanied Britton as a good-luck charm. As with so many people attached to the Susanna Dickinson story, there is no accounting of Britton after that.

For reasons that can only be guessed at, Britton gave the Travis ring to DeWitt Anderson, a comrade-in-arms in the Confederacy, who wore it until he died in 1902. T. H. McGregor, a relative, then became its owner. His son, Douglas, donated it to the Alamo museum in the 1950s. The ring was encased only feet from the spot where Travis had hung it around Angelina's small neck some 115 years earlier, and it remains there today.

According to local lore, Angelina followed the army camps for awhile during the Civil War. She later returned to Galveston, where she died on July 13, 1869, at the age of thirty-five. There are no markers in Galveston for the "Babe of the Alamo," however. A hurricane hit the island in 1900, killing more than six thousand people and wiping out the graveyard where Angelina was interred.

As for Susanna, she left Houston in 1857 and showed up in Lockhart, a small community near Austin, in Caldwell County. This move proved to be the turning point in her life. The troubles she had lived through in Houston were behind her. In Lockhart she established a reputable boardinghouse. Not long thereafter, she entered into her fifth marriage, to German immigrant Joseph William Hannig, sixteen years her junior. From

Joseph Hannig —Courtesy Texas State
Library and Archives Commission

all reports Hannig was an honest, hardworking, shrewd businessman. He was skilled in woodworking, a trade that would serve him well.

Susanna sold her land holdings. With the money, she helped Joseph set up a cabinet shop in Austin. The couple moved to a small, rather plain house on Pine Street (now Fifth Street), between Neches and Red River. In Austin the Hannigs invested in land, flour mills, and a furniture store, and ran a mortgage operation. They became entwined in the social life of the bustling, fast-growing metropolis. Joseph concentrated his trade on furniture and undertaking. In the late 1870s Susanna and Joseph built a two-story frame home on the northeast edge of the city, at today's Duval and Thirty-second Streets. The house, situated on a high piece of ground, afforded its occupants a view of the city in one direction and vast growths of vegetation in the other.

Susanna Hannig, survivor of the Alamo and of life, grieved over the early death of her daughter and was often wracked by horrible memories of those days in March 1836. Still, she managed to enjoy her later years. She took part in the society of a thriving new capital in a thriving new state, financially secure, at last with a husband who loved her.

On April 27, 1881, while in San Antonio on business, Susanna, now sixty-six, visited the Alamo again. Though it was not a public appearance, the *San Antonio Daily Express* reported on the visit. Susanna, the article stated, had tears in her eyes as she related the memories she had carried for forty-five years. Her feelings "came back as vividly to memory as though her experience of yore had been but yesterday."

Susanna's health began to decline in 1883. On October 7, 1883, at age sixty-eight, she died from what was termed hemorrhage of the bowels. She was buried in Oakwood Cemetery in Austin. Joseph remained in the city long enough to assure that Susanna received a proper burial with a marker appropriately placed on her grave. He then returned to his business interest in San Antonio, a furniture store he had opened some years earlier. In 1884 he married Louisa Staacke. Six years later, suffering a serious case of gastritis, Joseph died at his home on June 6, 1890. His body was returned to Austin for burial beside Susanna, per his request.

Although a picture of Susanna Dickinson was hung in the Alamo in 1929, it was not until 1949 that the state of Texas installed a marker on her grave denoting her contribution to history. In 1976 the legislature, leaving her interment in Oakwood undisturbed, placed a marker in the state cemetery in Austin, at last assuring her recognition as one of the early heroines of Texas.

Had Susanna been able to write, she might have left a wealth of information about the people at the Alamo—Travis, Bowie, Crockett—and of those immortal thirteen days. As it is, a void remains in our knowledge of Susanna, her daughter, the "Babe of the Alamo," and that old musty mission still standing in the middle of San Antonio.

Maybe that's the way it should be. Mystery leads to legend. The Alamo and what happened there in 1836 was destined to become a legend, while the surviving eyewitness to that saga created her own legend, through silence.

2

Francisca Alavez

THE ANGEL OF GOLIAD

On March 6, 1836, some 189 men died behind the crumbling, pockmarked walls of the Alamo, a San Antonio mission, in what would become the most re-membered battle for Texas independence. Stories would be told and retold, movies made, and pictures painted of the great effort by a handful of men against an army of fifteen hundred-plus (estimates vary up to five thou-sand) well-trained, well-equipped soldiers, extolling the Texians' gallantry in a gallant time.

Three weeks later, in a presidio known as La Bahía, in the little town of Goliad, ninety-three miles south-east of the Alamo, 342 men were executed on orders of the same man who had laid siege to the Alamo, Gen-eral Antonio Lopéz de Santa Anna. No movies have been made of this massacre, few stories are told of its happening, and the men did not die heroes. The sol-diers died due to indecision and incompetence. Their leaders failed to carry through on their orders, orders issued from a conflicting, confusing provisional government of a republic that was not yet a reality.

Yet out of the Goliad debacle emerged a story of bravery, defiance, and near sainthood in the form of one young, beautiful Mexican woman, Francisca Alavez, known in the annals of Texas history as the "Angel of Goliad." This would be the only recorded incident where a Mexican, crossing the Rio Grande with the Mexican army, ever showed compassion for the avowed enemy of the homeland.

Little is known about the background of Francisca (her name is variously spelled and she is also called Panchita) Alavez. She entered the Texas independence story when General José Urrea, one of Santa Anna's best officers, crossed the Rio Grande in February 1836. On the general's staff was a Captain Telesforo Alavez. There is conflicting evidence on whether Francisca was a camp follower, Alavez's lover, or his wife. While she did carry the captain's name, there is no proof they were ever legally married. The survivors of the Goliad tragedy described Francisca as no more than twenty years old, dark-haired and very beautiful.

The settlement of Goliad had been known as La Bahía, Spanish for "the bay," a name that referred generally to Matagorda Bay. At the time of Anglo-American colonization, in the 1820s, La Bahía was one of three Spanish settlements then in Texas, the other two being Bexar (now San Antonio) and Nacogdoches, near the Louisiana border. In 1829 the name La Bahía was changed to Goliad, with the former name retained only for the presidio. It was at the Presidio La Bahía that the first declaration of Texas independence was read, albeit prematurely, on December 20, 1835.

One of the main characters in the Goliad story was James Walker Fannin Jr., born in Georgia and educated at West Point. In autumn 1834 he moved with his wife and children to Texas to establish a plantation. From the moment of Texas's first agitation for independence, Fannin was one of its biggest boosters. He entered the fray in August 1835 and remained in the struggle until his death seven months later.

Fannin showed great courage and leadership, along with James Bowie, in the defense effort around San

La Bahía Mission —Courtesy Daughters of the Republic of Texas Library

Antonio in late 1835, and shortly thereafter as a recruiter for the emerging Texian army. It was a few months later, at La Bahía, that the thirty-year-old Fannin was to become a hero or a fool, depending on one's historical tilt.

Fannin was sent to Goliad as part of the Matamoros Expedition, which General Sam Houston later aborted. Under Fannin were two volunteers, James Grant, a Scottish-born physician active in Texas politics, and Francis W. Johnson, a Virginian who had come to Texas for his health. Johnson, too, soon became involved in Texas government, and he had been in charge of the Texian militia that took San Antonio from Mexican forces in December 1835. Fannin sent Grant and Johnson south toward Matamoros to prepare for the invasion.

Meanwhile, unknown to the Texians, Santa Anna had laid plans to stage a two-front siege on the Alamo. One of his most able and trusted officers, General José Urrea, was to move to Matamoros and from there cross into Texas. The Texians were confident that Mexico posed little threat to their own territory, so they were lax in security and in following military procedures. They would soon pay dearly for these oversights.

Johnson and Grant had divided their forces at San Patricio, fifty miles southwest of Goliad. Johnson remained there while Grant rode toward Agua Dulce, twenty miles southwest. On February 27, Urrea surprised Johnson at San Patricio. The Texian leader had posted no sentries. All the volunteers except Johnson and five others were killed or captured in the assault.

Urrea then moved toward Agua Dulce in search of Grant and his men, whom he attacked on March 2. Grant and all but six of his men were killed or captured in the seige.

When General Houston learned that Santa Anna had crossed the Rio Grande and was just twenty-five miles south of San Antonio, he instructed the men at the Alamo to vacate the mission. When they refused, he ordered Fannin to reinforce the garrison there.

Fannin, unaware of the fate of his two subordinates, started for San Antonio with about 330 men, but he was short on wagons and horses. As the company attempted to cross the San Antonio River, two miles from the presidio, three of the wagons broke down, and it was only through extreme good luck and hard labor that the men transported four cannons across the stream. The ammunition wagon remained on the Goliad side. It was then that Fannin received news of Johnson's defeat. He decided to return to Goliad and prepare that site as a defense against the approaching Mexican army.

The men busied themselves with reinforcing "Fort Defiance," as Fannin had dubbed the presidio. A short time later, they received another directive to send additional troops to San Antonio to assist Travis. Two days after that, as they prepared for the march to San Antonio, Fannin received news of Grant's defeat. To make events even more confusing in the constantly changing scenario, Fannin received new orders from Houston. With the fall of the Alamo on March 6, the commanding general now directed Fannin to move his army east, to Victoria, to establish a defensive position there. He was instructed to take only the artillery and stores that could be moved expeditiously and without delay, and to sink the remainder in the San Antonio River.

With the Mexican army now in close proximity, civilians in the area between Goliad and Victoria began moving out. Fannin sent Captain Amon King and Colonel William Ward to aid the settlers in their evacuation, but Urrea took both officers and their approximately eighty-five volunteers prisoner. These men were later marched to Goliad, where the captured Fannin troops soon joined them. Meanwhile, Fannin, still in Goliad, awaited the return of Ward and King—it wasn't until March 17 that Fannin learned of their fate. Still, Fannin hesitated to vacate his defensive position at the presidio to establish one in Victoria. This delay, plus the restlessness of the men under him, anxious for a fight with the Mexicans, ultimately led to the Goliad massacre.

On March 19, under cover of dense fog, Fannin finally ordered his men out of the fort. Their movement was slow on the roadless, barren plain and further handicapped by the trudging oxen pulling the wagons. Fannin had ignored Houston's order to carry only the artillery necessary for self-defense, taking along nine brass cannons and five hundred muskets. Compounding his poor decisions, he overlooked a very important item of materiel: rations for the men. Less than twenty miles from Goliad, the company was alerted to the enemy close behind.

As Fannin's men scurried toward a wooded area, the ammunition cart broke down and the soldiers found themselves in a depression in open land, surrounded by Mexican troops. The rebels gave a good account of themselves, however. They fought off the attackers from mid-afternoon until past dark. Though they were without water or provisions and short on ammunition, the better-equipped, better-led Mexican army failed to defeat them. General Urrea waited for the arrival of more artillery and additional troops.

The morning of March 20 found the Texians completely surrounded, with the Mexican force on a high hill overlooking their lower defensive position. With newly arrived reinforcements, Urrea now had about one thousand men, while the defenders had only about two hundred still capable of fighting. Their gunner had been killed, their engineer seriously wounded, and Fannin himself had been wounded during the melee.

The Mexicans rained shot upon the rebels from their lofty perch. It didn't take long for Fannin and his men to realize resistance was useless; continued fighting would only result in their deaths. Still, there was growing disagreement among the American officers whether to surrender or fight to the bitter end. Many were concerned about the reputation of the Mexican military for its barbaric retaliation on captured enemies. Only after firm agreement to an honorable surrender had been reached did the officers consent to Fannin talking with the other side under a white flag.

The Americans were under the impression that, under the terms of capitulation, their wounded would be adequately cared for and all private rights would be respected. The actual document, however, is open to a different interpretation. In article 1, Fannin surrendered his forces "at discretion to which the Mexican officers agreed." In article 2, the wounded, including Colonel Fannin, would be treated with all possible consideration. In article 3, the rebels were to be treated as prisoners of war and placed "at the disposal of the Supreme [Mexican] Government."

The perils of article 3 become clear when the dictates of the Mexican government, i.e., General Santa Anna, are brought into focus. A decree had been set forth in Mexico City that foreigners captured with arms were to be regarded as pirates and executed. Santa Anna had taken pains to emphasize this provision to General Urrea, who, himself more soldier than terrorist, was reluctant to follow this ruthless policy. Urrea and some of his officers agreed that Fannin and his troops surrendered in good faith, certain that the Mexican government would deal with them in a humane, compassionate way. Some historians believe that Urrea promised the resistors he would use his influence with the Mexican government to have the execution decree set aside for the Americans.

Once they surrendered, Fannin and about 240 of his men were marched back to Goliad as prisoners. The rest of the Americans, about 80 in number, were wounded and could not march; they were transported to Goliad later. Urrea notified Santa Anna of the conditions under which the Americans had surrendered and recommended clemency. Santa Anna quickly and angrily refused, ordering all prisoners at Goliad (both Fannin's men and others) to be executed immediately.

The acting commander at the Presido La Bahía was Colonel José Nicholás de la Portilla. General Urrea had moved on to Victoria, and from there he sent a letter asking Portilla to treat the prisoners with compassion and respect. Portilla, no more a butcher than Urrea, was, nevertheless, a soldier, and he knew he had to follow the dictates of his president.

On the morning of March 27, Portilla ordered the prisoners dispersed from the presidio in three different directions. The Americans were led to believe they were being marched from their place of confinement to a central point distant from the presidio, where they would be set free to return to the United States. When the captives tromped out of the fortress, they were in good spirits and full of hope.

One group of captives was marched northward, toward San Antonio; another eastward, along the road to Victoria; and the third headed south, on the San Patricio road. About three-quarters of a mile from the fortress, in each direction, the guards stopped their prisoners. When their leaders gave commands quickly in Spanish, many of the captives realized something bad was afoot. The guards encircled the prisoners, raised their rifles, and fired. The first volley killed all but a few of the Texians. Some ran, but they were pursued and most of them either shot or stabbed. Miraculously, a number managed to escape. Some fled into the woods along the San Antonio River; others feigned death and escaped when the guards returned to La Bahía.

Fannin was put to death within the walls of the compound along with about forty other wounded men who had been kept inside the fort. Fannin had reconciled himself to death and requested that he not be shot in the head and that he be buried. He was shot in the head and thrown on a pile with other slain prisoners. The bodies were burned.

The best estimate of the victims of the Goliad massacre is that twenty-eight managed to escape the execution squad outside the presidio and twenty were spared because they were physicians, nurses, interpreters, or mechanics who could serve the Mexican army. Another twenty or so survived thanks to Francisca's intervention. Of those marched from the presidio, an estimated 342 met their maker.

For sanitary reasons, the Mexicans attempted to burn the bodies at the presidio, but the green mesquite wood made this almost impossible. Those farthest from the compound were left to the buzzards and wolves. It wasn't until June 3 that Texas General Thomas Rusk sent a party to the area to secure the remains and bury them. Today, a monument stands where Fannin and his men are buried, in the largest mass grave on American soil.

Amid the sounds of violent death, another voice cried out on that fateful day from the San Jacinto Plain. The number of deaths at Goliad would have been even

The Fannin Memorial at Goliad —Author photo

higher had it not been for the courageous intervention of Francisca Alavez.

Francisca's first intercession in the Texian cause came when the Mexican army, led by General Urrea, occupied the small settlement of Copano, now long deserted, in today's southern Refugio County. An American ship from New Orleans, the *William and Frances*, carrying sixty-eight volunteers led by Major William P. Miller, docked at Copano Bay. The hot, restless men, unaware that Copano was in Mexican hands, jumped into the water and swam ashore, only to be greeted by armed and angry Mexican soldiers. Although some of the Americans tried to pose as tourists, the Mexicans weren't fooled and took the new arrivals prisoner. The Americans were tied up, more stringently than necessary, and left in the hot sun without food and water.

This was Francisca's first encounter with "gringos," and she was less offended that they were enemies of her country than she was at the harsh treatment they were receiving. She raged at the guards to untie the prisoners and give them food and water. The Mexican soldiers hesitated at first to give comfort to their enemy. But Francisca's insistent demands, coupled with the fact that she was an officer's wife, soon wore them down.

The Americans were most grateful to the lovely woman for her intervention and quickly expressed their feelings with smiles and words of appreciation. The gratitude of the men impressed her, and from that day forward she would be a thorn in the side of her patriotic, aristocratic husband.

Francisca accompanied Telesforo as he escorted American captives to Goliad. Along the way, she became friendly with one of the American soldiers. Upon her arrival, she came face to face with the presidio's "Black Hole," where over four hundred prisoners were crammed into a room so small there was no space in which to lie down; bodies were held in place by other bodies. When Francisca saw these wretched conditions, she went immediately to Colonel Portilla and talked him into letting the captives move into the courtyard for room and fresh air. She also persuaded him to give them food and let the American doctors treat them.

Francisca knew the fate of the prisoners, especially considering Santa Anna's hatred for gringos. The day the order came to execute all prisoners, Portilla allowed Francisca to see it. She knew the post commander had no choice but to follow instructions. Portilla's admiration for the bravery of the young woman showed when he allowed her to talk him out of executing the men captured at Copano Bay. Her justification, that they had never fired a shot against any Mexican national or soldier and had taken no part in the Texian rebellion, convinced him. Portilla shipped those men to a prison in Matamoros.

The night before Portilla was to execute the prisoners, Francisca, under cover of darkness, smuggled a dozen of the captives onto the mission parapet, where she kept them hidden until after the massacre. One source claimed that the enterprising woman managed to pull off this feat by wearing a soldier's overcoat (which she supposedly secured with the assistance of the sweetheart of one of the troopers).

The following morning Francisca, along with several other Mexican women, all dressed in black, stood outside the presidio and watched as the men, unsuspecting, were marched to their deaths. She wanted to do something but was virtually helpless. Suddenly, noticing a fifteen-year-old boy in the line of march, Francisca pulled him from the ranks, telling the officer in charge that she needed him in the hospital. The officer offered no objection, but the lad made an effort to rejoin his comrades. Like them, he had no inkling of what lay ahead. But for Benjamin Franklin Hughes of Kentucky, the unit's drummer boy, Francisca proved to be an angel: that night, he was one of the few Americans still alive in Goliad. Hughes later settled in Dallas, where he lived the rest of his life. Some forty years after the Goliad affair, he wrote an article affirming the massacre and attesting to Francisca's role in saving his life.

The American doctors were spared, but this exclusion did not extend to their relatives. When Francisca learned that the son of Dr. John Shackelford (for whom Shackelford County, Texas, is named), had been executed, she cried. She asked Dr. Shackleford, "Why wasn't I told you had a son here? I would have saved him at all hazards." Shackelford later escaped from the Mexicans and eventually returned to Alabama. His account is probably the most complete and the most reliable of the Goliad massacre.

Among the prisoners who managed to escape was William Hunter, a volunteer from New Madrid, Missouri. Hunter was apparently left for dead after being shot and bayoneted at the end of the death march. He stated that after a time, a beautiful lady named Alavez dragged his body to the brush on the banks of the San Antonio River and dressed his wounds.

At one point, after the Goliad executions, Mexican soldiers came upon seven of the escapees. They killed three of them and took four alive, who were later sent to Victoria. By this time, Telesforo Alavez had been reassigned to Victoria as part of Urrea's entourage, so Francisca was there when the four prisoners arrived. One of them, Isaac Hamilton, described what transpired when they were lined up in the market square in front of a firing squad. Brazenly, if not wisely, Francisca threw herself in front of the line of Americans. Her bravery caught the emotions of another Mexican woman standing among the onlookers and she joined Francisca. When the two refused to move, the execution was canceled.

On April 21, 1836, a momentous date in Texas history, General Sam Houston led his rabble force across the San Jacinto Plain and routed General Santa Anna and his men. Knowing that once the victorious Texas army was regrouped it would head south to liberate that part of the new republic, General Urrea moved his men across the Rio Grande, into Matamoros. Telesforo Alavez was among the retreating troops, and Francisca accompanied him.

By some records, shortly after the army's arrival in Matamoros, Telesforo went to Mexico City and there abandoned Francisca. There are claims that the captain was something of a scoundrel and that he had another wife, Maria Augustina de Pozo Alavez, whom he had abandoned along with their two children in 1834. She wrote the Mexican Ministry of War in 1837, asking for assistance in getting support from Alavez. It is known that Telesforo remained in the Mexican army and retired as a colonel after almost forty years of service. There is nothing more of his private life on any official record.

There is evidence that Francisca returned to Matamoros, homeless and penniless. Some claim she was accepted by many of the locals for her kind past actions, and she continued to take an interest in the American prisoners in Matamoros until they were freed several months later. That Francisca was solicitous toward the American prisoners is believable, considering her past actions and apparent innate compassion. That she was welcomed among her countrymen, however, is doubtful. Residents south of the border had little, if any, sympathy for Texians. It is difficult to believe they would overlook the treachery of someone who helped renegades.

A more credible account of Francisca Alavez's story came to light in the 1930s. Mrs. Elena Zamora O'Shea, a teacher at the Santa Gertrudis Ranch (part of the vast King Ranch empire of south Texas) in 1902 and 1903, wrote in 1936 of an incident that bore on the legend of the Angel of Goliad. According to Mrs. O'Shea, every Friday after class, two old Mexican men, one named Alfonso, a servant at the King Ranch, the other called Don Matias Alavez, would come to the schoolhouse and listen as she read from Spanish newspapers and lessons from the children's books. One day, as Mrs. O'Shea read aloud about the incident at Goliad, Alavez became visibly excited. Afterward, he told the teacher of his family.

Alavez said that his grandfather was Telesforo Alavez. Telesforo was brought up in the old Mexican tradition, in which families arranged marriages. He had no love for the bride his parents chose for him, and the two separated after a few years. The church granted an annulment but forbade remarriage—in other words, no divorce. Telesforo met Francisca shortly after his annulment and fell in love with her.

Disregarding the rebuke of both church and family, Francisca and Telesforo ran off together. When the army sent Telesforo to the Rio Grande frontier in northern Mexico, Francisca went with him. After the Texian insurrection, Francisca and Telesforo settled in Matamoros. It was only Telesforo's prestige that kept the townspeople civil toward Francisca, since many Mexicans deeply resented her benevolence toward the gringos. When Telesforo died, however, she was immediately shunned.

Two children were born of the couple's union, a boy named Matias and a daughter, Dolores. Matias, feeling that his mother should get away from the ostracism, crossed the Rio Grande and took a series of ranching jobs in Texas. In 1884 Captain Richard King, who knew both Telesforo and Francisca, offered Matias a job and the family moved to his spread. Francisca died at the King Ranch and is buried there in an unmarked grave.

Descendants of Francisca are still associated with the King Ranch. Many have become doctors, businessmen, government leaders, and military officers. The Alavez name became a part of the Cavazos clan, which includes Lauro Cavazos, one-time president of Texas Tech University and later Secretary of Education under President George H. W. Bush. Another Cavazos connection to the Alavez family is U.S. Army four-star general Richard O. Cavazos.

Bust of Francisca Alavez at the Presidio
La Bahía Museum —Author photo

The compassion and humanity Francisca Alavez showed toward an enemy of her country is remarkable, especially given that her actions threatened her husband's career and her own safety and made her a pariah among her own people. No greater or more sincere tribute can be made than the one written by a man who was saved by this courageous woman: "God bless her. She saved my life and the lives of my companions."

Today in the graying, haunted halls of La Bahía stands a bust of Francisca Alavez. The Angel of Goliad is the only Mexican in the Texas struggle for independence to be honored by Texas. Even in the coldness of the bronze, the woman's stamina, determination, courage, and compassion shine through.

3

Emily Morgan

THE YELLOW ROSE OF TEXAS

General Antonio Lopéz de Santa Anna, president of Mexico, crossed the Rio Grande River in February 1836 and headed north for a fortified mission in the sleepy little town of San Antonio de Bexar. There was vengeance in his heart for the hated gringos of this northern Mexico territory after the recent embarrassing capitulation of General Martín Perfecto de Cos, his brother-in-law. Not only had Cos lost the fortress known as the Alamo, he had surrendered a military force of eleven hundred officers and men to a motley, rebellious crew of Texians totaling no more than 350 untrained, undisciplined so-called soldiers!

Santa Anna, the self-proclaimed "Napoleon of the West," had vowed to run every Anglo renegade out of Texas, back across the Sabine River into the United States. If things worked the way he planned, there would be little running and much bloodletting. The Mexican troops arrived at the Alamo on February 23, and after a thirteen-day standoff, victorious Mexican troops stood

General Antonio Lopéz de Santa Anna —Courtesy
Daughters of the Republic of Texas Library

in the mission compound surveying the carnage. They had put down the rebellion. Or so they thought.

Following the sacking of the Alamo, the Mexican dictator headed east, chasing the upstart Texian government and makeshift army. The defenders of the Alamo, in delaying Santa Anna, had given General Sam Houston a little time to make some kind of a regimented force out of a bunch of craftsmen, farmers, and soldiers of fortune. No one really expected the motley band to defeat or even deter the organized and well-equipped Mexican army. Yet, a little more than a month after the fall of the Alamo, the Texians met and defeated the Mexicans at San Jacinto.

The battle took a scant eighteen minutes. The Texians lost nine men dead with twenty-three wounded. Mexican losses were unbelievable for such a short battle: 630 killed, 750 taken prisoner. It was not only one of the most surprising defeats in the annals of military history, it also ended the Texas war of independence.

What accounted for this unlikely outcome? Beyond the Texians' quest for freedom and thirst for revenge for the Alamo, there was an additional ingredient both serendipitous and provocative. The pinch of spice in this Texas saga was a beautiful young mulatto woman, now venerated in historical record where she was once revered only in song.

Emily West, later to adopt the family name of Morgan, was born near Albany, New York, around 1816. Although a freed woman, she traveled to Texas as an indentured servant to Colonel James Morgan. Originally from Pennsylvania, Morgan migrated to Texas from North Carolina in 1830. He had contracted with a firm in New Orleans to open a mercantile business in the territory. He acquired a good deal of acreage around Harrisburg, now part of the city of Houston. At the mouth of the San Jacinto River, at a site later called Morgan Point, Morgan laid out the town of New

Washington, which would soon become the seat of the fledgling province.

Morgan staunchly supported the Texas Revolution both financially and personally. Designated a colonel in the Texas army, he was assigned to defend the island of Galveston, and he and his troops set about building fortifications there to repel the Mexicans.

Morgan was away at this station when Santa Anna arrived at New Washington. There the general spied a beautiful young mulatto woman helping load supplies at the dock. She was getting Morgan's family ready to join him at Galveston. The womanizing dictator immediately decided that Emily Morgan was to be his new "personal maid," and soon the lovely twenty-year-old occupied his resplendent, candy-striped, three-room tent.

In the meantime, Houston maneuvered his troops in various twists and turns, leading the Mexicans first in one direction, then another, but always staying far enough ahead to avoid attack. This constant evasion of confrontation frustrated both the provisional Texas government and Houston's men, who were eager to fight. When he turned his army south at Harrisburg and headed for the coast, however, the rebels were relieved. He was moving toward a battle.

Houston took his men to the west side of Buffalo Bayou, in present-day Houston. Santa Anna, close behind, camped in an enclosure three-fourths of a mile from the Texians. A rise in the ground was all that prevented the two armies from standing eyeball-to-eyeball. To assure that this was the final confrontation between the two forces, Houston ordered the only bridge connecting the bayou to the mainland blown up; there was no escape for either army.

The Mexican general was flagrantly scornful of the Texians. He refused to order enough guards or set up any type of a rampart for protection. Even when his officers advised against such negligence, Santa Anna turned a deaf ear. Apparently he had dallying with Emily, not military strategy, on his mind. Outfitted in a medal-bedecked uniform topped with a Napoleon-style hat, Santa Anna paraded the perimeter of his camp in open view of the Texas army. This was not only a display of defiance toward his enemy, but probably also the bantam rooster strutting for his female.

The Mexican strongman had chosen the wrong woman this time. Emily was a Texian sympathizer. Shortly after leaving New Washington, Santa Anna ordered a slave named Turner, whom he had taken at the same time he acquired his new maid, to perform a reconnaissance of the rebel army. Before Turner and his escort of soldiers left on their mission, Emily secretly had a word with him. Because Captain Morgan kept his family apprised of rebel activity, Emily knew where Houston's company was camped. She also knew Turner would be sympathetic to the Texians. She disclosed Houston's whereabouts to Turner, instructing him to tell the Texian leader that the Mexican army was in hot pursuit.

Through guile and good horsemanship, Turner was able to pass on Emily's warning. He attempted to help the Texas cause further by relaying false information to Santa Anna about Houston's location, but the other scouts told the Mexican leader of the Texians' real movements. Thanks to Emily and Turner, Houston was able to continue his hide-and-seek game until he was ready to call the shots. A few days later, he had his opportunity, saying "fight and be damned."

When Houston moved his force into battle formation at four-thirty in the afternoon on April 21, 1836, all was quiet in the Mexican camp. The soldiers were enjoying a siesta, with rifles stacked and a limited guard at the edge of the camp. Their leader was at his tent, which had been situated on a romantic spot overlooking San Jacinto Bay. Inside was a stolen piano, silverware, china, food, and chests of opium to sate the dictator's addiction. Texian spies reported that Emily was serving Santa Anna a meal in front of the tent.

By the time the Texians moved in, Santa Anna had retired into the tent with Emily. At the first sound of gunfire, the general ran out, stumbling over cases of champagne he had stacked at the entrance, clad only in silk drawers and bright red slippers. Mass confusion overtook both his officers and his troops. Santa Anna, unable to restore order and mount a defense, wrapped himself in a bed sheet and, after grabbing a box of chocolates and a gourd of water, jumped on a horse named Old Whip and vanished into the woods.

The following day James Sylvester, a Texian soldier, captured some Mexican escapees during a search. Imagine Sylvester's surprise when he marched into camp with

"Surrender of Santa Anna" by William Henry Huddle
—Courtesy Texas State Library and Archives Commission

his captives and heard the other Mexican prisoners begin chanting, "El Presidente! El Presidente!" Sylvester had captured Santa Anna, clothed in the uniform of a common soldier.

The Texians wanted to hang their defeated adversary on the spot. There has been speculation that the Mexican general flashed the bonding Masonic sign, readily recognized by Houston, as a fellow Mason, and that is the reason his life was spared. It would appear more reasonable, though, that the pragmatic Houston knew Santa Anna would serve no purpose dead. As Mexico's president he had the power to make and enforce a peace treaty and order the remainder of the defeated army back across the Rio Grande.

El presidente was arrogant during his captivity, demanding comforts for himself that he had refused Texian prisoners. He denied he had ordered attacks on Goliad and the Alamo (although he had been at the latter, in his resplendent uniform), and he attempted to lay blame for the Mexican defeat at San Jacinto on subordinates, all the while chewing plugs of opium to garner courage. During his four-month imprisonment at Patton (later Hogg) Plantation and then Orozimbo Plantation, near present-day West Columbia, Santa Anna became despondent. On one occasion he swallowed poison; the quick action of plantation owner Dr. James Phelps, who pumped his stomach, saved him.

Another Lone Star legend is attached to Santa Anna's imprisonment. After Mexican loyalists discovered their leader's whereabouts at the Orozimbo Plantation, they decided to attempt a rescue. As the men crept in late one night, they suddenly heard the terrifying baying of hounds. The noise continued unabated and eventually the rescuers-to-be were frightened away.

Yet there were no dogs, housed or strays, at the Orozimbo Plantation. The guards at the plantation, who also heard the racket, had an explanation for the sound: The baying was not hounds, but the hellish cry of ghosts—the ghosts of the victims of the Goliad massacre. And so was born the legend of the "Ghosts of Goliad."

In an interesting aside, a few years later, after his release, Santa Anna would be the catalyst for the creation of a worldwide treat. In 1865 the ex-general was in New

York hawking valueless Mexican bonds. He had also brought with him some *chicle*, the dried sap of the sapodilla tree, and he attempted to persuade inventor Thomas Adams of its value as a substitute for rubber. Adams experimented with the substance, but it was unsuccessful as a rubber substitute. He hit upon another idea. At the time, paraffin was used as the base of chewing gum, but it was a poor ingredient. Perhaps chicle would make a better gum. The experiment worked, and Adams's chewing gum, Chiclets, rewrote mastication history.

After the battle at San Jacinto, Emily Morgan was escorted back to New Washington, some eight miles away from the battlesite, by a member of the victorious Texas army. She told Colonel Morgan of the miraculous victory, and he later learned of the important role she had played in the event. Her actions so impressed the patriotic Morgan that he immediately released her from indenture. It is rumored that he bought her a home in Houston, in a community of free blacks. Later, she returned to New York, where she faded into oblivion.

Emily's exploits were only hinted at for some time after the battle. But folklore picked up on the heroics of this woman soon thereafter. An Englishman, William Bollaert, a frequent visitor to Texas and an acquaintance of Morgan's, kept a diary of his travels and recorded Emily's deeds. However, the diary was not made public until around 1902. By then the legend of the Yellow Rose had already become part of Texas lore. The story was given even more credence when Mexican historians admitted to Santa Anna's "quadroon mistress" during the Texas campaign.

Emily Morgan's story inspired "The Yellow Rose of Texas," one of the best-known songs about Texas. Originally a Negro folk song created shortly after the Texas Revolution, it has undergone changes since its inception. A line in the chorus, "She's the sweetest rose of color, this darky ever knew," was later changed to the more palatable "She's the sweetest little rose that Texas ever knew." Sung during the Civil War and both World Wars, the song was made even more popular in the 1960s when band leader Mitch Miller featured it on one of his "sing-along" television shows.

There is some contention that Emily might not have been at San Jacinto with Santa Anna. It has been proffered that the Mexican leader's ineptness was due more to his opium habit than his sexual appetite. Yet historical records support her presence, and Texas tradition supports her contribution.

Santa Anna, despite his many faults, was a charismatic and skilled leader. He had the men, the experience, the equipment, and the time to easily defeat the puny, unprepared Texian troops. If he had devoted his attention to matters at hand at San Jacinto, there is little doubt that the Texians would have failed, at that time, in their quest for independence. The history of Texas, the United States, and Mexico could have been far different. As it happened, Emily's beauty and desirability completely turned Santa Anna's head for that important moment. For this, Texas and the United States can be grateful.

As long as there is a Texas, and as long as the melody of "The Yellow Rose of Texas" lingers, Emily Morgan and her part in that short-lived battle on April 21, 1836, will be remembered.

4

Lottie Deno

SHE "DEALT" WITH THE BEST OF THEM

The Wild West truly existed at Fort Griffin in the late 1800s. First established in July 1867 on the banks of the Clear Fork River, the fort was moved due to flooding to a rise that overlooked the Clear Fork Valley. The town of Fort Griffin sat at the foot of the military camp on flat land between the hill and the river. Because of its location, soldiers usually referred to the town, such as it was, as the Flat.

Situated on the San Antonio-Dodge cattle trail, which saw more than 100,000 cattle cross the trail in 1876 alone, the town was host to cowboys, buffalo hunters, outlaws, gamblers, soldiers, Indians, and fallen women. More people were killed on the streets of the Flat in its short lifetime than in the entire history of Dodge or Tombstone. In a span of twelve years, thirty-five men were killed in open gunfights, and almost that number were found dead of unexplained—and uninvestigated—causes, sometimes the result of a "vigilance"

Sketch of Fort Griffin by unknown artist
—Courtesy Texas State Library and Archives Commission

committee. Soon Fort Griffin earned the moniker "Town of Babel" for its wickedness and wildness.

The Flat, like modern-day Las Vegas, never closed. It was a noisy, dirty, lawless place, with more than a dozen saloons, gambling parlors, dance halls, and some four hundred permanent residents eager to relieve cowboys, businessmen, soldiers, and anyone else entering the town of their money. There were several houses of ill repute, which were allowed to operate as long as the fines, usually about one hundred dollars a year, were paid on time.

Into this den of iniquity a young, good-looking woman called Lottie Deno arrived one day on the Jacksboro stage. Lottie Deno was not her real name, but in that place and time privacy was respected and claims were seldom questioned. Lottie looked and acted a cut above most of the women of the Flat. She dressed conservatively, never drank alcohol, and was never heard to use a curse word or utter a foul remark.

Lottie rented a small shanty on the edge of town. Only a select few ever entered the house until the day she left. Even in a place like the Flat, pillars of the community existed, and the women in that caste shunned the new arrival. This bothered Lottie not one whit, and she mostly maintained as much distance from them as they did from her.

Lottie Deno was born in Warsaw, Kentucky, south of Cincinnati, on April 24, 1844. At least one source lists her birth name as Carlotta J. Tompkins. Her father owned race horses and indulged in gambling. It was from him, by one account, that Lottie acquired her agility with cards and her nomadic tendencies.

Of fine polish and an excellent education, Lottie was bred for success. But it all went up in smoke with the occurrence of two events: the death of her father, killed in his first battle in the Civil War, and the destruction that war wrought on her family's fortune. The plantation was lost and the family was left with few convertible assets. As the elder of two daughters, Lottie bore the responsibility for her mother's and sister's survival. Lottie decided to venture to Detroit, where friends of the family would take her in. Good Southern families lived there, and Lottie hoped to meet and marry a suitable young man who would return with her to Kentucky and take over the family business.

In the northern environment, Lottie's beauty and Southern culture made her an attractive and popular guest at dinners and parties. Lottie decided to try her luck at the gambling tables and soon became an accepted member of a private club in Detroit. She was good enough to support herself as well as her mother and sister, sending the latter to a reputable finishing school. Though Lottie was achieving what she had set out to do, she became tired of smoky rooms and gambling halls. Her eyes, like those of many others, turned west.

At this time Johnny Golden, a fellow gambler from the genteel class, came into Lottie's life. He was younger than she and a Jew, but, despite her conservative upbringing, neither fact concerned her. The two teamed up and worked the riverboats, plying the Mississippi River as they meandered their way west.

Mary Poindexter, a former slave from her Kentucky plantation, accompanied Lottie on her odyssey. Mary was a large woman, reportedly pushing seven feet in height. Completely devoted to Lottie, she went everywhere with her mistress. Once, when the two of them were walking along the Mississippi River near New Orleans, Mary suddenly dropped to the ground, throwing herself over a coiled rattlesnake ready to strike. When the snake bit Mary, Lottie hurried her back to the boat, but there was little the doctor could do. Mary recovered, but she eventually lost an index finger. Lottie never forgot Mary's bravery and sacrifice.

Another time, Lottie was approached by a past gambling opponent who felt she had been less than straight in dealing cards. When he came close to Lottie with an angry expression on his face, Mary grabbed him with her strong arms and sent him swimming in the river.

On the riverboats Lottie, with her grace and beauty, became a favorite at the gaming tables and was quickly accepted by the regular card-playing clientele. An expert player, she more than held her own with the best of them. Johnny Golden, on the other hand, was less fortunate. They decided to split up and meet later in San Antonio, Texas.

In the meantime, Lottie's financial burden was lifted somewhat, albeit sadly, by the death of her mother. She continued to support her sister in finishing school. Wishing to avoid any embarrassment to her sibling, who was in a fine eastern seat of learning, Lottie pretended her affluence came from a wealthy husband.

In New Orleans, Lottie plied the casinos. In time her winnings were sufficient to finish paying for her sister's education and to get herself and Mary to San Antonio in comfort. When they arrived in the Alamo City on June 1, 1865, they took the place by storm. Lottie's exquisite features, gorgeous red hair, fine figure, and smooth, cultured ways made the menfolk gasp. She stayed a few months in Mrs. Adams Boarding House and later rented a small house on San Pedro Street, near the center of town.

Lottie became a social butterfly in San Antonio and was accepted among the city's higher class. Mary made acquaintances that kept her informed of when and where the latest gambling soirees were taking place, though

*Lottie Deno,
circa 1860s*
—Courtesy
Hunter family,
Bandera, Texas

Lottie did not participate right away. She maintained a distance from dives and other sordid gambling parlors, patronizing only the best clubs.

It wasn't until October 1865 that Lottie made her first appearance at a San Antonio gambling establishment, the Cosmopolitan Saloon. She made quite an impression the first time she walked in, dressed in the finest silks, with Mary strolling confidently behind. Mary was allowed to sit near her mistress during the games, a fact resented by several players. The resentment soon passed, however, as Lottie's talents won the admiration of the club members.

Lottie didn't limit herself to the Cosmopolitan. Many other fine and reputable clubs opened in San Antonio during her residency, and she frequented most of them: the Comanche Club, the Jockey Club, the Jack Harris Saloon. Lottie was so popular that she became known as the "Angel of San Antonio." She was hired to deal for the University Club, the most fashionable gambling bistro in town. The University was owned by the Thurmond brothers, Frank, Bob, and Harrison. Frank would enter Lottie's life again later.

Lottie stayed at the University three years and might have remained longer had not Johnny Golden appeared on the scene. While no proof exists that the two were ever involved romatically, he apparently had some emotional effect on her because once he showed up, her winnings started dropping. Golden announced that he wanted to team up with her again, as they had done on the Mississippi boats, but Lottie had no desire to reestablish their connection. Some speculated that she was in love with Frank Thurmond. Their alleged affair was curtailed, however, after Thurmond killed a man in a knife fight and was forced to flee San Antonio. He remained a fugitive for some ten years.

The more Lottie's fortunes declined, the more restless she became. Her interest was piqued when she heard about the easy pickings at Fort Concho and Fort Griffin, in northern Texas. She believed a move would not only give her a chance to replenish her coffers, it would also rid her of some excess baggage, namely, Johnny Golden.

Meanwhile, Mary had come to love San Antonio and the friends she had made. She might have become involved with one of several San Antonio female gangs who took in orphaned children and taught them to steal. Mary was distressed to learn that Lottie planned to leave. One night, while her mistress dressed, Mary disappeared, taking her few possessions with her. She was never seen or heard of again. When Lottie Deno, the "Angel of San Antonio," departed the Alamo city, it was without her beloved and devoted companion.

Lottie's arrival in the stark, woman-hungry outpost of Fort Concho, near today's San Angelo, quickened the pulse of many men there. Her beauty and bearing spoke volumes, and she uttered little and revealed nothing of herself or her past, not even her name. She created much mystery and was dubbed "Mystery Maud" by the editor of the local newspaper. Lottie rented a small adobe house on Concho Street, and residents wondered why such a stunning woman was in a hole like Fort Concho. Their bewilderment was soon appeased.

One night, after the gambling dens had come to life, Lottie walked into a saloon, her high-fashion dress and good looks bringing a hush over the gathering. After she sat down at one of the tables, the patrons soon discovered why she had come to town. Although women rarely entered saloons in those days, Lottie soon won the men over with her dexterity with the pasteboards.

While Lottie was admired and accepted by the male population of Fort Concho, the womenfolk, envious of her good looks and popularity, wagged their gossipy tongues endlessly. The veil of mystery that Lottie purposely wrapped around herself brought on many wild rumors, none of which she ventured to squelch: she was running from a husband that beat her; she was a member of European royalty, seeking thrills on the wild frontier; she was a lady of wealth from New Orleans society getting her kicks among the riffraff of degenerate towns.

After several months, Lottie took her gambling talents to Fort Griffin, also known as the Flat. In the Flat, less civilized than even Fort Concho, Lottie was definitely out of her element, yet she thrived and never let the town's sordid ways change her. She lived alone in a rented shanty on the edge of town. Few people ever penetrated into her private quarters, and those who did were upright citizens of the community, men who avoided the trappings of cheap saloons and gambling parlors. In the quiet of her small house, she would engage select individuals in the fine art of card play. There is nary a hint that the men allowed past her door ever participated in any activity other than gambling.

Lottie gambled in town, too, and was a house dealer at the Beehive Saloon. Once, while Lottie was dealing faro there, two nefarious gamblers got into an argument, each accusing the other of cheating. They drew pistols and fired, both at the same time. When the sheriff arrived on the scene, he found two dead bodies, most of the saloon's patrons scattered, and Lottie calmly sitting at the table counting her winnings.

It was in the Flat that Lottie acquired the alias by which she was best known. Not wanting to embarrass her relatives, she had never used the family name of Tompkins, content to let people call her what they would. One evening, after cleaning an opponent out of his poker stake, a drunk in the saloon called out, "Honey, with winnings like them, you ought to call yourself 'Lotta Denero.'" The drunk's comment served as the seed for the name she adopted and carried for many years thereafter.

The Flat saw some famous figures pass through. Doc Holliday and his woman, Kate "Big Nose" Fisher, gambled in the saloons there. Wyatt Earp, the lawman from Dodge City, and John W. Poe, deputy to Pat Garrett when Billy the Kid was killed, visited the Flat, as did Bat Masterson, the marshal of questionable reputation. Lottie played cards with these and other characters of the era. Once, Mike Fogarty, owner of the Beehive Saloon, where Lottie worked, lost all his money and the saloon itself to Doc Holliday. Lottie implored the famous gunfighter to give her a chance to recoup Fogarty's losses. Holliday, though a killer, was a gentleman of Southern breeding and agreed to the lady's request. When Lottie rose from the table a short time later, Fogarty once again owned the saloon and had back the three thousand dollars he had lost.

There was something more to this story as well. Mike Fogarty was, in fact, Frank Thurmond, Lottie's San Antonio lover.

The mystery of Lottie Deno is further muddled by the revelations of John C. Jacobs, buffalo hunter and onetime sheriff of Shackelford County. Jacobs professed to have personally known Lottie and claimed she confided in him. Supposedly she told Jacobs, among other things, her real name, but swore him to secrecy, an oath he apparently kept until his death in the mid-1930s. Though historical records support some aspects of Jacobs's version of Lottie's story, the information conlicts in other ways. Whether it was Jacobs or Lottie herself who bent the truth is impossible to say.

According to Jacobs, Lottie's father owned a stable of successful racehorses. One of the jockeys, name unknown, caught Lottie's eye and they fell in love. Against her parents' wishes, the pair eloped. Evidently they never forgave her. Even after Lottie's father's death, letters she posted to her mother returned unopened.

The jockey was a passionate gambler, and he was often in trouble because of it. As Jacobs's account goes, it was Lottie's husband who taught her the tricks of the trade. The couple drifted across the country, from New Orleans to Mobile, from Kansas City to Nashville, going from one casino to another, Lottie sharpening her skills along the way.

Lottie's husband, a man of violent temper, knifed a man during a card game one night. He fled town, alone, with all the money he and Lottie had stashed away, and set out for Mexico. He caught up with Lottie while she was living in the Flat and asked her to join him in San Angelo.

Though Lottie had reservations about rejoining her husband, she took the chance. She left the Flat on May 25, 1878, without saying a word to anyone. She took with her a small leather trunk, supposedly containing more than $25,000 in winnings she had reaped during her two years in the Flat.

It is possible that Lottie's jockey husband was Johnny Golden. If so, it would explain her distress at his sudden appearance in the Flat. Here the story takes another turn.

One day the Fort Griffin marshal and his deputy came to arrest Golden for horse stealing, a grave crime on the frontier. While Johnny denied he even owned a horse and said he had arrived in the Flat by stagecoach, the lawmen ignored his claims and proceeded to escort him to the stockade. Hardly had the three men exited the saloon when, according to the arresting officers, a mob accosted Johnny and killed him. Another version states that he tried to escape and was shot.

The explanation given by the lawmakers was accepted at face value. No investigation was ever conducted to challenge their word. Some residents believed that Lottie had a lover who paid the lawmen to dispose of Golden out of jealousy, but there is no evidence of such a conspiracy.

Shortly after Golden's death, Lottie left for parts unknown. She still must have felt a bond with him, because she paid for his coffin and a new suit to bury him in. After she left, the sheriff and a few citizens, hoping to solve the mystery of Lottie Deno, entered her deserted house on the outskirts of town. The only thing they discovered was a tastefully decorated two-room home, neat and orderly. Pinned to a pillow was a note in Lottie's handwriting: "Sell this outfit and give the money to someone in need of assistance."

For the people of the Flat, that ended the saga of Lottie Deno. She vanished as quickly and quietly as she had arrived, and the mystery that came with her, left with her.

Fort Griffin shut down a few years later, and the Flat faded away. But Lottie herself lived on. She next emerged in Kingston, a small village on the edge of Gila National Forest, in southwestern New Mexico. There Frank Thurmond was waiting for her, and over the next few years they opened a saloon called the Gem in Silver City, kept busy with various gambling endeavors, and bought and sold silver-mining claims and real estate. Playing both sides, Lottie and Frank grubstaked miners, then took their diggings at the poker table.

For the first two years Lottie and Frank passed as a common-law couple, even though the Territory of New Mexico had, in 1856, passed a law banning "concubinage." When, two decades later, local jurisdictions began enforcing the law, Lottie and Frank complied. They became man and wife on December 2, 1880, in Silver City. The register lists her name as Carlotta J. Tompkins.

In the ensuing years, Frank made many shrewd investments in real estate, mining, and other enterprises. In July 1885 he purchased a lot in a small community called Deming, about twenty miles north of the Mexican border and ninety miles west of El Paso, Texas. This would become home to Lottie and Frank for their remaining years.

Not too long after settling in Deming, Frank got into a fight and, as he had in San Antonio, killed a man with a knife. This time, however, witnesses verified that he had been provoked and no charges were brought against him. The incident served to quell Frank's wild streak, though. Both he and Lottie gave up gambling. He turned to mining, real estate, and ranching endeavors; she became the consummate homebody.

The reclusive Lottie became more sociable in Deming. She was a charter member of the Golden Gossip Club, a clique whose membership signified the blue chip of Deming womanhood. Playing cards (for match sticks) was the club's main focus, exceeded in fervor only by the gossip passed back and forth during meetings.

Frank Thurmond died June 4, 1908, at age sixty-eight, of mouth cancer. On February 9, 1934, Lottie passed on, just shy of her ninetieth birthday. No children were born of their marriage. Neither obituary mentions the past of these two figures. When she died, Lottie Deno was Mrs. Frank Thurmond, the name she accepted and carried for more than fifty years.

Few people reading the death notices had any hint who Charlotte Thurmond really was or the rowdy life she and her husband had led. One man in Deming at the time, however, would later bring the mystery of this unique woman and her remarkable past to light.

J. Marvin Hunter was born in Loyal Valley, Texas, March 18, 1880. His father, a teacher and newspaperman, placed young Marvin in the newspaper environment, a setting he never relinquished until his death in 1957. In 1900, at age twenty and newly married, Hunter arrived in town to start work at the *Deming Headlight*. He and his wife rented a small brick house on the corner of Spruce Street and Zinc Avenue. Behind the Hunters lived a couple named Frank and Charlotte Thurmond. In time, Hunter came to believe that Charlotte Thurmond was the fascinating Lottie Deno.

When Hunter first came to Deming, he had never heard of Lottie Deno. Shortly after his arrival, he began hearing rumors of the obscure, suspicious background of the Thurmonds. Yet there was little evidence that anything was amiss. Frank Thurmond was a rancher by trade, and both he and Charlotte were upright, active members of the community. Charlotte was a refined, kind woman who went out of her way to avoid unpleasantness. It was difficult for Hunter to picture this woman gambling in a saloon. But following a conversation with his employer, newspaper publisher George Shakespeare, Hunter became a believer.

Shakespeare attested that Frank Thurmond still turned a mean card and could empty the pockets of most gamblers of the day. As for Lottie, he said, she had given up gambling for high stakes, but had, in her time, roasted many a gambler. Shakespeare stated that he had personally seen Lottie take to the floor a wealthy man from back east, and he had even suffered from her expertise. According to him, Lottie used to be known as the "Faro Queen of Silver City."

With the dogged determination of a good newspaper-man, Hunter researched the story of this lady gambler. His findings left him no doubt that Charlotte "Aunt Lottie" Thurmond, as she was known in Deming, and Lottie Deno were one and the same. He established his case well in a small, readable book published in 1959 titled *The Story of Lottie Deno: Her Life and Times*.

The life of this extraordinary lady naturally led to fictionalization. Alfred Henry Lewis, a writer in the late 1800s and early 1900s, wrote a series of novels set in a mythical place called Wolfville. The stories revolved around two gamblers, Faro Nell and Cherokee Hall. It has been taken for granted that the two characters were unabashedly Charlotte and Frank Thurmond. The books were serialized in *Cosmopolitan Magazine* in 1901 and 1902. It is also thought that Miss Kitty from television's *Gunsmoke* and Laura Denbo from the 1957 movie *Gunfight at the OK Corral* were characterizations based on Lottie Deno.

Lottie made her mark in real life; the fiction merely gilds the lily. She turned cards with the best of men and enhanced her own enigma by keeping her secrets to herself. She made her place both in history and in lore. Long may her legend live.

5

Pamelia Mann

AS MEAN AS THEY COME

From about 1836, starting with the Texas Revolution, until the close of the nineteenth century, there existed between 95° and 125° longitude what some call the Wild West. The overwhelming majority of people moving west during America's great migration engaged in peaceable pursuits, carving out homes on a raw frontier; mining the goldfields of California, Colorado, Montana, and the Dakotas; running cattle along trails from San Antonio to Abilene and Dodge City. While there were rustlers and claim jumpers, highwaymen and con men, the bad guys were few in comparison to the honest folk of the time. Most people carried sidearms to kill rattlesnakes and hammer nails; seldom were there face-to-face confrontations in the middle of a dusty street at high noon.

The image of the cowboy—riding herd all day, whooping it up in saloons at night, compassionate deep down but always brave and fearless—was created by the dime-store novelists of the late nineteenth and early twentieth centuries, and perpetuated later by Hollywood. From these images, many of us envisioned ourselves riding alongside a large herd of cattle, heading north along the Chisolm Trail. In reality, living in the Wild West meant hard work, hard luck, and hard living. There was little glamour to it, and often little reward. Yet there were some real-life characters whose adventures were so extraordinary they make the fictional ones seem tame. One of these characters was Pamelia Mann, a Texas figure with few equals on the feminine—or the masculine—side of history.

Pamelia's deeds ranged the gamut from calling down one of Texas's most famous leaders, to repelling armed lawmen, to running houses of ill repute in the hellish days of early Houston. Her criminal record was probably longer than that of any man of the time. She cursed with such volume and velocity as to make the Texas sky as blue as it is today, and she just might have been the source of our dreaded "blue northers." An artisan with a knife and a gun, she was never without either. She had no fears and felt no loyalties.

Little is known of Pamelia's early life, which only adds to her mystique. It is believed she married twice before hooking up with Marshall Mann. Her first husband's name may have been Hunt, and her second, Samuel Ezekiel W. Allen. But with Pamelia little is certain. The few records available suggest she was born Pamelia Dickinson around 1800, probably in Kentucky. The first official record of her is on the birth certificate of the younger of her two sons, Samuel Mann, in Frankfort, Kentucky, in 1826.

Little information survives about Marshall Mann, either. He may have been born in King and Queen County, Virginia, around 1793. His brother, William, first chief justice of San Patricio County, Texas, was born there in 1816. There is no record of Marshall and Pamelia's marriage.

An article in the *News-San Antonio*, November 5, 1879, placed Pamelia in another territory. The article states that she was born in Tennessee, was an uncontrollable child, and ran away from home at age sixteen. She turned up in New York City, plying her feminine attributes in a brothel. Pamelia might have remained in New York had she not, in a fit of temper, pushed a coworker down a flight of stairs, breaking both her legs. Not wishing to face the law, she struck out for New Orleans. There, it's reported, she opened her own house of pleasure and named it Sure Enuf. Her reputation as a woman not to fool with became legendary. She always appeared wearing a pistol and carrying a Bowie knife.

One night a client mistreated one of the women in Pamelia's employ. When confronted, the man turned on the madam. Mistake. Pamelia shot him dead. Killing the man did not bother Pamelia until she learned that her victim was the son of a local judge. Gathering the large amount of cash she had accumulated, she and her husband, Marshall, along with her two sons, followed the path many others took at the time: GTT (Gone to Texas).

The San Antonio newspaper article is the only record of this part of Pamelia's life, but its validity is dubious. It goes on to tell of later escapades—her fall as a madam in Houston, her return to New York with a fortune, a final move to California—that find no support in other documentation.

When Pamelia and her family left New Orleans for Texas in 1833, they boarded a schooner headed west. The trip would not be simple. Due to the volatile political situation then existing between Mexico and Texas, Mexican officials had a blockade in force along the Gulf Coast. The schooner ran the blockade at Galveston Island and landed at Harrisburg. The Manns then followed the Brazos River to a spot near San Felipe, some forty miles west of present-day Houston, where they built a home in January 1834. Pamelia's elder son, Flournoy Hunt (also called Nimrod), was seventeen years old; Samuel was eight.

Here, in the wild and remote section of a republic in the making, Pamelia's grit and daring came to the forefront. One day, the driver of a wagon, hell-bent on maintaining a straight course through Pamelia's land, decided he would cut the fence blocking his way. Bad decision.

As the man was about to apply his ax to the fence, he heard a noise. Looking up, he found himself staring into the end of a long-barreled rifle, held by a boy. Not to be scared off by an eighteen-year-old, the driver returned to his wagon and pulled out his rifle. As he approached the fence, coldly eyeing the youngster on the other side, he was stopped in his tracks by a woman's cool but forceful voice coming from the nearby cabin. "Shoot him down, Nimrod," Pamelia admonished her son from the porch. "Blow his stupid brains out!"

The teamster took a different route.

Pamelia and Marshall ran a boardinghouse in Washington-on-the-Brazos during the 1836 Constitutional Convention, serving meals for $1.25 a day. When the convention adjourned in mid-March, Pamelia returned to San Felipe. It was about this time that her curious relationship with Sam Houston developed.

After Santa Anna razed the Alamo, the Mexican strongman headed east, chasing the Texian army under Houston. Along with Houston's soldiers marched local settlers, constantly moving to stay ahead of the oncoming Mexican army. Pamelia joined the movement.

Marshall's whereabouts at this time are unknown, but what is known is that Pamelia ended up in Houston's tent. She was even observed with the general's head in her lap while she combed his hair. It was the beginning of a mysterious relationship between Pamelia and Sam Houston, one that continued over the next few years.

As with other colonists heading for the U.S. border with Houston's army, Pamelia carried personal belongings and drove livestock, in her case two teams of oxen. At Groce's Point, on the Brazos River, the general's officers commandeered a yoke of her oxen to pull an ammunition wagon. Heavy spring rains had turned the

Sam Houston, circa 1837
—Courtesy Texas State Library and Archives Commission

dirt roads into muddy quagmires, and only oxen had the strength to tow the heavy cannons and ammunition wagons. Pamelia had no objection, because Houston had assured her that his army was traveling toward the American border.

Pamelia's willingness to lend her oxen abruptly ceased when Houston suddenly turned his army south, toward Harrisburg. Upon observing the general's alteration in course, she demanded the return of the oxen. Houston told her that the army needed them and refused her demand. In language that would turn a barroom purple, Pamelia informed the general that she didn't care how desperately the army needed the oxen, she wanted them back—and she would take them back! Whereupon she jumped from her horse, cut the oxen's harness straps, and led the animals off toward the border.

Houston's army witnessed this defiant act, and it was the only time they ever saw him bested. He let Pamelia leave and didn't order anyone to retake the beasts. The wagon master, Conrad Roher, was not as pliant. He told Houston he would get the oxen back and started out after Pamelia. The general called after him, warning him that she was a hellcat. Then, in mud to the top of his boots, he turned to help his men push the wagons out of the muck.

Later that night Roher rode back into camp with neither oxen nor Pamelia. There was evidence, though, that the two had met—Roher's shirt was torn, as was his dignity. When ribbed by fellow soldiers, his only defense was that Pamelia was more man than woman.

Houston's movement south culminated in the final battle of the Texas Revolution, on the San Jacinto Plain, on the afternoon of April 21, 1836. What had occupied the days and weeks of Pamelia's husband, Marshall, during those trying times is unknown. A few days after the battle of San Jacinto, he joined the Texas army, where he remained at least until the latter part of September 1836. Once the revolution ended, Pamelia, Marshall, and Pamelia's two sons were among the earliest occupants of the new city of Houston, arriving there by March 3, 1837. At Sam Houston's request, the city was named the capital of the Republic of Texas, a short-lived distinction.

Pamelia purchased Houston's first hotel, built earlier by Colonel Benjamin Fort Smith. The transfer of deed was made on June 8, 1837, and Pamelia renamed the place Mansion House. It soon became the city's top hotel and brothel, serving large amounts of coffee, tea, wine, and hard liquor along with meals. For her regular male clientele, Pamelia also provided female companionship.

Through the doors of Mansion House passed dignitaries, congressmen, and military leaders, including the heavy-drinking Sam Houston, as well as Tonkawa Indian representatives experiencing their first taste of the

One of the earliest known photographs of Houston, 1856, sixteen years after Pamelia Mann died and the Mansion House was sold.
—Courtesy Houston Public Library, Houston Metropolitan Research Center

white man's strange food and drink. The Indians, in Houston to sign a treaty with the republic, were put up in Mansion House at government expense.

One episode at Mansion House resulted in a duel between Dr. Chauncey Goodrich and Levi L. Laurens. Goodrich, Laurens, and several others shared a room one night—in those days single rooms were almost unheard of. Upon awakening, Goodrich discovered that a $1,000 note had been stolen from his wallet. Why he accused Laurens of the crime instead of another occupant is unclear. Regardless, the following morning the two men faced off in the street, and Goodrich shot and killed Laurens. The real thief, Marcus Stanley, was later caught attempting to cash the note in New Orleans. What happened to Stanley isn't known, but when the truth filtered back to Houston, an enraged citizenry ran Goodrich out of town.

Amid these goings-on, Pamelia expanded her business interests. She opened a livery stable across from Mansion House and purchased various real estate, including buildings. By tax time in 1837, she owned eight lots, four slaves, three horses, forty head of cattle, and five buildings. With other assets, her estate was valued at more than $15,000, an impressive fortune in those days. By 1840 her wealth had almost tripled, to $42,530, with 2,250 acres of land, ten lots, thirteen slaves, four horses, and ten head of cattle.

During their marriage, Marshall Mann occupied his time overseeing Pamelia's various business interests, especially running the livery stable. He also served as doorkeeper of the Texas congress when it was in session and established himself as an upright citizen of Houston. He was among a group of seven men appointed to serve on an interim police committee in June 1837. A year later, he contracted an unidentified illness and died on October 4, 1838.

While Pamelia had demonstrated flashes of brazenness in the past, her husband's presence apparently held her mostly in check. Shortly after his death, her run-ins with the law began. At least one of those clashes had an almost ludicrous tone.

Upon checking out of Mansion House, a certain doctor boarding there asked for a trunk he had left in safekeeping with Pamelia. For whatever reason, she refused to give it to him. The doctor reported the incident to local authorities, who issued a warrant for retrieval of the luggage. When a city constable presented the warrant to Pamelia, he was chased off under threat of bodily harm. Determined to follow through on his duties, the constable gathered a posse and returned to Mansion House. Pamelia, spewing forth language normally associated with teamsters, met the posse on the porch. As the lawmen approached there appeared a band of renegades, Pamelia's hired henchmen, who put the posse to rout, never to return.

Most people of the town were amused at the incident. Some, however, looked upon the episode with suspicion. Had the matron paid off the lawmen? Certain individuals decided to find out by setting up a sting. They left a trunk, supposedly containing a large sum of

money, in Pamelia's protection. When asked for its return a few days later, she refused. This time, the county
sheriff not only retrieved the trunk, he arrested Pamelia
for theft.

As the story goes, after Pamelia had a few words with
the sheriff, he decided to conduct the official investigation inside Mansion House. Pamelia plied the investigators with splendid refreshments and other favors, the
extent of which can only be guessed at. Nevertheless,
the judge on the scene found Pamelia guilty. Before
announcing the sentence, he declared a brief recess and
rode into town to settle some other matters. When he
returned to the hotel, he found a surprise.

Pamelia, indignant at being convicted after her "generosity" during the investigation, had closed the gates and
locked the hotel doors. Inside, she held the investigators
hostage. Pamelia had her band of thugs guarding the
premises. Deducing that discretion is the better part of
valor, the judge accepted Pamelia's demand that the
charges be dropped. No more was ever said about it.

Not all charges brought against Pamelia were as
farcical as these. The first congress of the Republic
of Texas had passed a law making forgery a capital
offense, in response to the numerous forged land titles
popping up. On March 22, 1839, a Harris County
grand jury indicted Pamelia for forgery, a charge lev-
ied by Mrs. Mary Hardy. Mrs. Hardy claimed her
husband had lent Pamelia $1,000 on March 1, 1836,
and she had a contract indicating the debt. When
Mrs. Hardy presented the note for collection, Pamelia

produced a receipt showing payment of the debt. The receipt was also dated March 1, 1836, reportedly signed by Mrs. Hardy and witnessed by William Barrett Travis. For someone as clever as Pamelia, this was a sorry ruse.

First of all, why would anyone pay off a loan the same day she borrowed it? Second, Mrs. Hardy would certainly have recognized her own handwriting. As for Travis's signature, Pamelia must have been aware that Travis was at the Alamo on the date in question; there was no way he could have witnessed the receipt.

Pamelia was incarcerated in the Harrisburg County (later changed to Harris County) jail. From the description of the jail, just being there was penalty enough. There were only two cells in the jail, plus what was known as the "debtor's room." Pamelia and other female prisoners were placed in the latter, but within plain sight of the cells occupied by male prisoners. The women were continually exposed to the men's leering and obscenities. While the language would have little offended Pamelia's sensibilities, even she must have suffered from the stench of the "night tubs," which were emptied only once a week.

When Pamelia appeared before the judge, she pled not guilty. She was represented by the law firm of Houston and Birdsall, to which she paid a fee of $1,800. John Birdsall, attorney general of the republic, handled the case. The trial began on May 17 and ended May 20. The jury convened for twenty-four hours. At least one juror considered some of the evidence circumstantial and argued for acquittal. At 7 P.M., May 21, the jury presented its verdict to the judge: guilty, with recommendation of mercy addressed to the court and to the newly elected Texas president, Mirabeau Buonoparte Lamar.

The jury, in its petition to the president, stated that "the peculiar situation of the accused, being a female, a mother, and a widow, and an old settler of the country" justified executive clemency and that the penalty for forgery was excessive and "bordered upon vindictive justice." Many citizens of Texas agreed with the jury's recommendation. Even one of the republic's newspapers took up the cause, calling for a reduction of the penalty for forgery.

On May 24, 1839, Pamelia appeared before Judge Benjamin C. Franklin. When asked if she knew of any reason why judgment should not be rendered, she remained silent. The judge remanded her to jail until June 27, 1839, at which time, between noon and two o'clock, she would be taken to the gallows and hanged. The sentence was never carried out. The following day, President Lamar pardoned her and directed the sheriff to set her free.

There is conjecture that Pamelia was falsely accused of the forgery, that she had been set up. She had very limited education and wrote even her own name with great difficulty, so for her to have forged someone else's name would have been nearly impossible.

Between 1837 and 1840, the courts almost became a second home to Pamelia. She was the plaintiff in seven civil cases and the defendant in eleven, an average of one case every two months. Of the seven suits she filed, she won five. In most cases, the reasons for these suits were not recorded, and the amounts awarded were not always recorded either.

As defendant, Pamelia was found liable in several cases. Mary Hardy, who had accused her of forgery, sued Pamelia twice and won both times. In the civil forgery case, the judge found that Pamelia was liable for the debt of $998 plus interest from March 1, 1836. Other judgments against her cost her hundreds more. Pamelia was cited twice for contempt of court but never fined.

Even Pamelia's personal life got her in trouble with the law. In addition to rumors about her involvement with Sam Houston, both before and after her husband's death, the widow was also seen with Tandy K. Brown, a man twelve years her junior, only a month after Marshall's passing. On May 13, 1839, the two were indicted for fornication.

While the case never came to trial, it may have put some pressure on the couple to make their relationship legal. On August 2 they secured a marriage license and signed a marriage contract, a forerunner of today's prenuptial agreement. Brown agreed that Pamelia could handle her property as she always had, without requiring consent or interference from him. They were married by the chief justice of Harrisburg County on August 4, 1839. Pamelia opted not to have a religious ceremony. Many people on the rebellious frontier felt religion had little relevance in their lives.

Unlike Marshall Mann, Brown shared Pamelia's criminal bent, and the back and forth with the courts continued. On May 7, 1839, Brown, Pamelia, and her son Flournoy Hunt were indicted for assault with intent to kill. The case never came to trial. On April 7 of the following year, Brown was charged with stabbing Ann Tucker, a freed black. There were no white witnesses and the charges were dropped. Later that same month, Pamelia and Brown were arrested and jailed for stealing Negroes, but the grand jury never indicted them.

Pamelia's son Flournoy tended toward aggression but never achieved his mother's notoriety. Nothing is known of Pamelia's younger son, Samuel Mann. On June 26, 1838, Flournoy married Mary Melvina Henry in a lavish ceremony at Mansion House, attended by many dignitaries of the day. Sam Houston served as first attendant, and many future leaders of the republic were there. Despite her wild and criminal ways, Pamelia was truly a social lioness, a leader in Houston society.

Flournoy's bride died less than three years after the wedding. On March 10, 1842, Flournoy married Elise R. C. Wilkinson, age fourteen. Soon afterward he joined a militia group called the Milam Guards and headed for San Antonio, but the army ordered him back almost immediately. Less than two months later, on May 7, at the Harrisburg racetrack, Flournoy got into an argument with a man named Black and was stabbed to death.

Two years earlier, Tandy Brown had contracted yellow fever and died September 7, 1840, at age twenty-eight. Pamelia died of the same disease two months later, on November 4. She was buried in an unmarked grave in the Old City Cemetery, later renamed Founders Memorial Park. Flournoy was appointed administrator of her estate and sold the furnishings of Mansion House at auction for around $2,652. Even before Pamelia's death, Mansion House had been in decline after Congress chose to move the republic's capital from Houston to Waterloo (soon to be renamed Austin, for Stephen F. Austin, the "Father of Texas") in 1839. Pamelia's other assets included seven slaves, some land, and livestock. Her debts totaled $3,512.

Thus ends the saga of Pamelia Mann. She could hold her own with any man and survived personal troubles and turbulent times. With sheer courage and daring, she met crises head-on. Her life was the stuff of legends.

6

Sally Scull

WOE TO THOSE WHO CROSSED HER

The crude, untamed frontier was an ideal setting for the birth of legends and myths. In the year 1821, with the first immigrants crossing into what was to become the state of Texas, the seeds of the great Lone Star legends were sown. These early Texans were adventurous and ambitious, entering a world unknown to them, a world of seemingly limitless opportunity and freedom.

It was in this time and place that Sally Scull, born Sally Newman, grew up. Sally probably could not have become who she was in Boston, Atlanta, Memphis, or New York, where she would have had to conform to the mores of civilized society. In Texas, however, she had free rein and lived a life unimaginable for most of us, man or woman.

Sally was born in Illinois in 1817, the fifth child of Joseph Newman and Rachel Rabb Newman. Her parents followed her maternal grandparents from Illinois to Missouri to Arkansas. They ended their travels in southeastern Texas, where both generations became part of Stephen F. Austin's "Old Three Hundred" and in December 1823 received large land grants in what are today Fayette, Colorado, and Wharton counties.

The Rabbs and the Newmans settled on the far western fringe of early Texas, and they experienced more Indian trouble there than did settlers farther east. In one incident an Indian—probably Comanche or Apache—was attempting to remove the front door from the Newman's cabin while Rachel and her daughter were inside. As the man tugged at the door, he let his foot slide into the open space underneath. With a swift swing of an ax, Rachel rendered the intruder toeless. On another occasion, when some Indians were attempting to enter the cabin through the chimney, Rachel struck a match to a feather pillow and tossed it into the fireplace. Sally must have taken after her mother.

On September 24, 1833, when she was sixteen, Sally registered the brand for the cattle she had inherited from her father, who had died two years before. Though she noted on the application that she was the wife of one Jesse Robinson, she registered the brand under her maiden name, an early indication of the independence she showed the rest of her life.

In 1833 Sally and Jesse presumably lived as man and wife and perhaps had a marriage contract. Due to a shortage of Catholic priests in the area, however, they didn't have a formal religious ceremony until March 31, 1838. Sally's marriage to Jesse Robinson, eighteen years her senior, endured for ten years, although it was not a happy union. The couple had two children, a girl, Nancy, and a boy, Alfred. In 1843 Jesse filed for divorce, asserting that Sally was a hellion to live with, a shrew of the worst sort. Sally countered with her own charges that Jesse often deserted his family, leaving the children's care and support to her. She declared in no uncertain terms that "Damn it, I want a divorce, too!"

Sally seemed to be on firm footing, since Robinson's second wife sued for divorce on the same grounds. Yet that did not stop the judge, in an almost unheard-of decision for the time, from awarding custody of the children to Jesse. Some time after the divorce, Sally "kidnapped" her daughter, but the court ordered her to return the child to her ex-husband.

Eleven days after her divorce, on March 20, 1843, Sally married George H. Scull (sometimes spelled Skull). She would have three more husbands after Scull but would forever carry his name. The couple had a ranch outside Goliad, and it was during this marriage that Sally developed her love for and interest in horse trading.

Little is known of George Scull, other than the contention that Scull was not his real name. It is believed he ran away from a wife in New Orleans and joined the Texians in their fight for independence. As the story goes, he fought with Fannin at Goliad and escaped the massacre with only a head wound. Contributing this miracle to the thickness of his skull, he made a play on the word and chose Scull as his new last name.

The Sculls divorced in either 1847 or 1848. Some say George returned to New Orleans, and others claim

Indians killed and scalped him. Either of these may be true.

On October 17, 1852, in Nueces County, Sally Scull joined John Doyle in holy matrimony. While little is known about Doyle and his eventual demise, there are stories. One account has it that Sally and her spouse were crossing the Mission River at Refugio on a ferry when John slipped and fell into the river, drowning. As onlookers murmured in horror over the tragic accident, Sally stood shaking her head. "Damn the man," she reportedly swore. "I just want that forty dollars he had in his pocket."

Another story raises speculation that Sally did her third husband in. John Salmon Ford, a Texas Ranger affectionately known as Rip, wrote in his memoirs of an incident at a place known as Kinney's Tank, near Corpus Christi. Ford was deep in thought when he was startled by the sound of gunshots. Looking up, he saw a man fall to the ground. A woman stood calmly nearby with a pistol in her hand. Ford, like everyone in south Texas, knew of Sally Scull and recognized her. Witnesses declared the shooting justifiable, and Ford did not arrest Sally for murder. Since this event occurred while Sally was married to John Doyle and nothing was heard of him again, some assumed that he was the victim.

Sally's fourth husband was a man by the name of Isaiah Watkins. As with her other mates, little is known about him factually, yet there is plenty of hearsay and speculation. According to one source, around 1858 Sally and Isaiah were staying in the Union House, a hotel in Corpus Christi. The couple had enjoyed a gala fandango the night before and Sally was sleeping late. Isaiah had tried several times to awaken her, but she wouldn't stir. Anxious to get started on their planned journey north, he impatiently grabbed a pitcher of water and threw it in her face. Sally, in a stupor, grabbed one of the pistols she always kept within fingertip reach and in one shot laid her fourth husband to rest. Following the mores of the day, the shooting was declared accidental and Sally was set free.

There are several variations on the story of Isaiah Watkins's untimely demise. Another version submits that Isaiah stuck his head in a whiskey barrel for a drink and Sally, fed up with his boozing, held his head in the vat until he drowned. Still another rendition claims that Sally forced her husband to drive a herd of horses across a swollen stream, and he got caught up in the swift current, swept from his horse, and drowned. Sally's reaction? She shrugged and continued pushing the animals across the river.

While Sally was losing husbands she was gaining a reputation for marksmanship. Whether in long skirt or pants, she always wore a bonnet and had two pistols belted to her waist. Her renown with the latter bordered on the mythic. She was a dead shot with both pistol and rifle, in either hand. One witness to her firearms expertise stated, "Them two big old six-shooters she packed didn't seem to bother her a bit. I've seen her put her finger through the trigger guard of a pistol, whirl it around and around, then catch it and fire at some object and she never missed." As many people learned the hard way, Sally was equally adept with Bowie knives and bullwhips.

Never called beautiful, Sally was often described as having features etched by the sun and wind of south Texas. Her steely blue eyes were said to have made many a man back down. Weighing 125 pounds at most, this dynamic woman made her imprint on a land already rampant with heroes and legends.

Sally was a true product of the restless West, and she often settled disagreements the way most men did: with force. On one occasion, after word crept back to Sally that a man in town was spreading rumors and making unkind remarks about her, she confronted him on the street and demanded an apology. Not to be dressed down by a woman, especially with onlookers nearby, the man arrogantly refused. In response Sally whipped a pistol from her holster and taught the man some new dance steps. Before losing a toe or two, the man quickly apologized to the fine lady, and the dance lesson ceased.

As this episode shows, Sally met people on her own terms, eyeball-to-eyeball, asking no quarter and giving none. Furthermore, she had honor. Her word was her bond, and she expected no less from others. One incident in particular illustrates this. A man named Drowdy had owed Sally money for some time. One day she ran into him and demanded he pay the debt, but despite her cussing and ranting, Drowdy wouldn't come across with the money. Hopping down from her wagon, Sally grabbed an ax and gestured toward the man's wagon train. "You hand over [the] money or I'll cut off the front wheel of every damn wagon you got." Sally's reputation, the ax in her hand, and the stare in her cold blue eyes convinced Drowdy she meant business. One debt erased.

Sally's rough language was almost as notorious as her talents of persuasion. Once, while hauling cotton along a muddy Texas road, she came upon a wagon hitched to two stubborn mules bogged in the mire. The man at the reins, unbeknownst to Sally, was a member of the cloth (although it would have mattered little had she known). Try as he might, the man could not get the mules to move. Sally stood by silently for a few moments, watching the agonizingly futile proceedings. Anxious to get her own wagon moving, she let fly a string of profanity that must have scorched the preacher's ears. Extolling the mules to move, her words had the desired effect: the wagon was soon on its way. A few miles down the road, Sally came upon the same scene again. This time, when she approached, the preacher begged her to use her profuse vocabulary to once more set the mules moving. She obliged.

In addition to Sally's impressive command of English, she spoke the Tex-Mex dialect as if it were her native tongue. When she wasn't traveling alone, she rode in the company of several Mexican *vaqueros*, or ranch hands, whom she controlled with an iron hand. With them, she roamed the territory between the Sabine River and the Rio Grande, making her headquarters at a small settlement called Banquete, about twenty miles west of Corpus Christi. At the Rio Grande, often under questionable circumstances, she gathered droves of horses and steered them to Louisiana, where she sold them. After a foray into borderland Mexico, she always returned driving a nice herd of stock, yet her money belt would be no lighter for the acquisition.

Horse trading was Sally's primary business and a profitable one. She did not merely manage her operation, she worked in the field. Her vaqueros, in fact, were hard put to match her pace. She could outshoot any of them, she roped and rode with the best of them, and she could drive a herd better than any of the wranglers in her employ. The vaqueros who worked for her and other Mexicans who knew her called her "Juana Mestena," Mustang Jane. Once, while driving horses, Sally's vaqueros refused to cross a rain-swollen river. Without hesitation, Sally maneuvered her horse into the stream, holding her guns aloft. The cowboys sheepishly followed with the herd.

Sally played as hard as she worked. She was an avid poker player and could be found in the company of many of south Texas's renowned gamblers. Her favorite haunts included both the elegant and the dingy: Old St. Mary's Saloon at Copano Bay, select gaming houses in Refugio, and a place known as Pancho Grande's in Corpus Christi. She also liked to dance and graced many a fandango with her presence.

Traveling south Texas, Sally knew all the ranches in the region. Ranch wives sometimes hinted that while

Sally made eyes at the menfolk, her vaqueros were busy cutting the best horses from the herd. There were also rumors that Sally cavorted with the Comanches and that they assisted her in her horse trading. If she admired certain horses but the owner refused to part with them, Comanche raiders mysteriously visited the ranch shortly after Sally's departure. Yet no one ever caught Sally in possession of a horse for which she couldn't show rightful ownership. This fact is not surprising, however, considering she never let anyone inspect her herds.

Sally's exploits sometimes led to trouble. On one trip, around 1860, Sally ran afoul of Juan Cortina, a Mexican Robin Hood. She was returning from Mexico with a herd of horses when Cortina, for reasons unknown and being a law unto himself, captured Sally and took her to Matamoros, where he threw her in jail. After five days he set her free, returning her guns and horses. We can only speculate on the reason for Cortina's generosity. Some believe Sally struck a deal with the Mexican rebel, possibly a trade of horses for her freedom. Maybe her Mexican contacts persuaded their countryman to release her. Just as credible is the theory that she won her release in a poker game with her captor.

By 1860 Sally had married her fifth and last husband, Chris Horsdorf. A scoundrel without redemption, Horsdorf was so despised by those who knew him that he acquired the derisive sobriquet "Horsetrough." Not surprisingly, the couple's union was no happier than Sally's previous ones.

During the Civil War, Sally's knowledge of the southern Texas backcountry served her well. Cotton was king in those days, and Sally could travel blindfolded along what became known as the Cotton Road. But Union forces had installed a blockade of Texas ports, stopping all shipments to England, the South's primary market. Fortunately, the United States was not at war with Mexico, so, according to international law, the Union could not block ports south of the border. This gave Texas an easy alternate route.

Seeing opportunity, Sally sold her stock of horses, bought wagons, and turned her vaqueros into cotton haulers. During the war years, Sally's wagons became a common sight on the roads from San Antonio to Matamoros. They hauled the cotton three hundred miles south, then filled the empty wagons in Mexico with supplies to carry back to inland settlements in Texas. Sally's enterprise also provided the Confederacy with much-needed money. When the war ended in 1865, Sally sold her wagons and resumed the horse business.

Sally's death, like her life, is rife with controversy. By some accounts she breathed her last in late 1865. She and her husband, Chris Horsdorf, had left for the border to purchase horses. Sally, as was often the case, was carrying a large sum of money. Some time later, Chris returned but Sally didn't. It was believed that he killed her for the money and buried the body somewhere between Corpus Christi and the Rio Grande. Postal carrier Matt Dunn supported this story, claiming he discovered the body on his route.

A different rumor said that Sally had wanted to rid herself of Chris Horsdorf because she was tired of supporting him. He was willing to leave but wanted a goodly portion of her estate, a request she of course refused. When he confronted her and she told him what he could do with his demands, he blew her head off with a shotgun.

Other reports have Sally selling horses to German settlers in Fayette County in 1879 and 1880. She was also supposedly seen driving cattle up the trails to Kansas in the 1870s.

Historical marker dedicated to Sally Scull at the Refugio County Museum
—Courtesy Refugio County Museum

As for Sally's two children, their fate is no more certain than their mother's. It is believed that Sally's son, Alfred, lived with his father, Jesse Robinson, on a homestead on Ramerania Creek, about fifty miles northwest of Corpus Christi. The elder Robinson remarried and fathered eight more children. It is doubtful he and Sally ever again came face-to-face. What finally became of Alfred is a mystery.

Sally reputedly had more contact with her daughter, Nancy. Determined that Nancy never suffer the hardships she experienced, Sally sent her to one of the best boarding schools in New Orleans. When Nancy returned to Texas, she married and lived up to her mother's dreams. Mother and daughter were allegedly close for a time, until one day, when Sally rode up to Nancy's house for a visit. One of the dogs on the premises growled at her, whereupon Sally pulled a pistol from her holster and silenced the dog forever. So ended the mother-daughter relationship.

The dog incident could have been the springboard for Texas mothers cajoling their children to behave "or Old Sally Skull will get you."

Some speculate that Sally's life would have been different had she retained custody of her children. As it was, she defied all expectations of womanhood in her own era or any other. Stubborn and determined, Sally Scull walked tall in a world of strong men and made anyone in her path step aside.

7

Sarah Hornsby

PROPHET OR DREAMER?

On a hot August day in 1833, Texas settler Josiah Wilbarger and four other men were scouting territory near present-day Austin when they spotted a lone Comanche and gave chase. The Indian eluded the party, and Wilbarger and the others turned back toward neighbor Reuben Hornsby's cabin, six miles away. The sun was high overhead when they decided to stop to eat and to rest their mounts. They paused by a small stream, and three of the men—Wilbarger, Tom Christian, and a man named Strother—unsaddled and hobbled their horses. The other two, Haynie and Standifer, leery of the Indian they had encountered, decided to leave their horses saddled and tied them loosely to a nearby tree. This precaution soon saved their lives.

The men started a fire to cook some beef, pulled some cold corn pone from their saddlebags, and passed it around. As they relaxed by the cool water they chatted and smoked. Suddenly, the sound of war whoops, rifle fire, and the swish of flying arrows shattered their serenity. The men jumped behind some trees and began firing at their attackers, a raiding party of about fifty Indians.

The spindly trees, typical of those in the central Texas region, offered little protection. Strother and Christian were killed almost instantly. Haynie and Standifer, who had left their mounts saddled, made a mad dash for the horses. Wilbarger, arrows in both his legs and a bullet wound in his hip, called after his comrades and ran in their direction.

As they mounted their steeds, Haynie and Standifer turned just as Wilbarger took a shot in the back of the neck. They saw the bullet exit through the front of his throat, blood spurting. He fell to the ground and was immediately surrounded by Indians. The two escapees spurred their horses and headed in the direction of Hornsby's cabin. They knew there was no use trying to help their friends. They saw the Indians with their knives and knew what would come next.

The Comanches worked fast. They scalped Christian and Strother, cut their throats, and stripped them of their clothing. When they set on Wilbarger, they saw that his throat was bloody from the gunshot and wasted no time cutting it, but they did scalp and strip him. As quickly as they had arrived, the Indians left. All fell silent.

When Haynie and Standifer arrived at the Hornsby home, they sent a rider on to the Wilbarger residence, some miles away, to relay the sad news to Josiah's wife, Margaret. By the time men arrived from the surrounding area to help, it was too dark to retrieve the remains for burial. They would have to wait until daylight. As everyone slept that night, Reuben Hornsby's wife, Sarah, suddenly awakened from a dream that left her trembling.

Sarah woke her husband and told him of the vision. In the dream she saw Josiah Wilbarger, naked, leaning against a tree. She said the dream convinced her he was alive and waiting to be rescued. Reuben scolded his wife for waking him, reminding her that he and the others had to get up early the following morning. He informed her, in no uncertain terms, that there was no way Josiah or anyone else could have survived the attack. Haynie and Standifer had seen Josiah bleeding from the neck with the Indians gathered around him. It was standing Comanche practice never to leave victims alive, cutting their throats to be certain they were dead. But her husband's skepticism failed to deter Sarah from the conviction that her dream was a premonition. She reluctantly went back to bed.

Within a short time the dream returned, exactly as before. Sarah was no longer to be placated. She awakened her husband and the other men. As she served them breakfast, she admonished them that her dream was an omen: they would find Josiah exactly as she had envisioned.

At the first sign of daylight the men mounted their horses. Before they departed Sarah handed three bedsheets to her husband. She instructed him to place one over Christian and another over Strother. The third was to wrap Wilbarger. Sarah further directed that Wilbarger be brought back to the cabin, where she could tend to his wounds.

While Reuben Hornsby had expressed some skepticism over his wife's dreams, he was less cynical than the others. He doubted that they would find Wilbarger alive, but he knew his wife was not given to irrational thinking. The mother of ten, Sarah had survived the rigors of frontier life and had had more than her share of experiences with Comanches. She had seen young boys killed and scalped, and she had buried the victims. Once, while her husband was away, she and a female visitor scared off a band of Indians by donning men's clothing and walking around the yard with Reuben's gun. Clearly she knew the realities, yet she was certain the nearly impossible scenario in her dream was real.

Reuben Hornsby and the others rode in the direction of the attack site, on the lookout for Indians. When they arrived, they immediately came across the bodies of Christian and Strother. They buried the two men, then searched for Wilbarger. They were puzzled when they didn't find his body with the others. They were certain he had been killed, but where were the remains?

Just as they were about to give up the search, one of the riders spied what he took to be an Indian leaning against a tree. From what he could see, the man was naked and covered with red war paint. He called out to the other men that he had found one of the Indians. When he raised his rifle, the man rose and held up his hands. "Don't shoot," he said, stumbling toward them. "It's Wilbarger."

Though scalped, wounded in half a dozen places, and near death, Wilbarger was just as Sarah Hornsby said he would be: leaning against a tree, awaiting their arrival. His rescuers gently wrapped him in the sheet Sarah had provided, and Reuben held him in his arms as they slowly rode back to the cabin.

Sarah, confident that Wilbarger would be found alive as she had dreamed, waited with hot water, bear's oil, and poultices at the ready. She nursed him for several days until he recovered sufficiently to be moved back to his home. Since he was in no condition to ride a horse or withstand the bumpy ride of a wagon, they transported him home on a makeshift sled. After a miraculous recovery, Josiah Wilbarger lived for almost a dozen more years.

After his rescue, Wilbarger described his ordeal. The bullet that passed through his neck served to temporarily paralyze him, and he couldn't wage any resistance to the Indians as they attacked him. This was lucky for him—had they known he was still alive, the Indians would surely have killed him. The paralysis prevented him from feeling any pain as the Indians roughly stripped away his clothing over his wounds, but he was fully alert and felt the flesh torn from his body as they scalped him. He said that it sounded like distant claps of thunder when they jerked the skin from his skull.

After the Comanches left, he fell into unconsciousness, not waking until late in the afternoon. The paralysis had left him and the pain from his wounds set in. Overcome with a tremendous thirst, he managed to crawl the few feet to the creek. He remained in the cold water until he was numb. Slowly, with agonizing pain, he crawled out of the steam onto a sunny spot on the ground, where he immediately fell into a comatose state.

When he next awoke it was almost nightfall. He had a faint remembrance of being scalped, but it didn't penetrate his consciousness until he became aware of blowflies swarming around, feasting on the open flesh of his head. Next he realized the Indians had stripped him completely—almost. For some reason, they left him with one sock. He pulled it off and, after shooing away the flies, covered his head with it.

His senses now orderly, he decided to try to make it to Hornsby's. He managed only about six hundred yards before collapsing. Capitulating to the inevitable, he leaned against a post-oak tree and awaited his fate. At that particular moment, it mattered little whether that fate would be rescue or death. Death seemed more likely, if not from his wounds, then from the wolves he heard howling in the distance.

After his rescue, while he was being tended at the Hornsby home, Sarah told him of her dreams. He looked at her, astonished. He then revealed something that had happened to him the night of the attack, as he listened to the wolves howl and awaited his death.

While he was leaning against the tree there appeared before him a vision of a young woman whom he recognized immediately. It was his sister, Margaret

Clifton, who lived in Florissant, Missouri. She spoke softly and kindly to him. "You're too weak to go on, brother dear. You lie here and rest and help will come to you before another day is over." She then turned and headed in the direction of Hornsby's cabin. He called after her, but she continued on, without turning around.

Weeks later, Wilbarger received a letter from Missouri. It said that his sister Margaret had died the day before the Indian attack. Had his vision been a delirious hallucination or a ghost?

Josiah Wilbarger believed he saw his sister's spirit that night, and that she not only gave him the courage to hold on but also alerted others, through the dreams of Sarah Hornsby, that he was alive. Sarah certainly believed her dreams, waking her husband twice that night to inform him of what she had seen.

Sarah's dream and Josiah's vision became the talk of the area. People who knew both Josiah and Sarah attested to their mental soundness and honesty, and they believed their stories.

Though Josiah Wilbarger recovered from his wounds, his scalp remained exposed for the rest of his life. His wife sewed caps for him from pieces of her silk wedding dress, and he wore them until he died. For twelve years after the attack, he operated a cotton gin and did pretty well. One day, walking through the building, he hit his head on a low ceiling beam. For most people this accident would have resulted in no more than a large bump. But for Wilbarger, the mishap was fatal.

He died on April 11, 1845. Both he and his wife were reinterred in 1932 in the state cemetery in Austin.

On the corner of Fifty-first and Berkman Streets in Austin is a monument marking the estimated site of the scalping. At Hornsby Bend, in Travis County, near Austin, is the Hornsby Cemetery, where Sarah Morrison Hornsby was laid to rest in 1862. Baseball Hall of Famer

Josiah and Margaret Wilbarger
—Courtesy Bastrop County Historical Society Museum

Rogers Hornsby, a descendant of the pioneer Hornsby family, is also buried in this cementery.

Josiah Wilbarger is one of the few survivors of a scalping. Would he have lived without the dreams of a woman down the road?

Grave marker of Reuben and Sarah Hornsby —Author photo

SITE OF THE HOME BUILT IN 1832 BY
REUBEN HORNSBY
(1793 – 1879)
AND HIS WIFE
SARAH MORRISON HORNSBY
(1796 – 1862)

SECOND BUILT IN "AUSTIN'S LITTLE COLONY"
FIRST IN THE PRESENT COUNTY OF TRAVIS

FAMED FOR CHRISTIAN HOSPITALITY

HERE JOSIAH WILBARGER RECOVERED
AFTER BEING SCALPED IN 1833

MR. HORNSBY AND HIS SONS FOUGHT IN
MANY INDIAN BATTLES AND SERVED
AS SCOUTS IN CAPT. JOHN J. TUMLINSON'S
COMPANY OF RANGERS
WHICH WAS ORGANIZED HERE IN 1836

Erected by the State of Texas
1936

8

Diamond Bessie

THE MYSTERY LINGERS

One of the biggest tourist draws in Jefferson, Texas, population 2,000, is its annual reenactment of the Diamond Bessie murder trial. The murder is still listed as unsolved, and the circumstances surrounding it and the subsequent trial and appeal remain a source of rumor, speculation, and folklore to this day.

On Friday, January 19, 1877, a man and woman arrived in Jefferson by train from New Orleans. They checked in to a hostelry called Brooks House, signing the registry as "A. Monroe and wife." That afternoon and the next day, the couple promenaded around Jefferson dressed in their finest garb. The woman, whom the man addressed as Bessie, drew admiring glances as the pair strolled the streets of the east Texas town. Because of her flashy jewelry, the townspeople took to calling her "Diamond Bessie."

At the inn on Saturday night, there was a loud and ugly disagreement between Mr. and Mrs. Monroe. The man in the next room, W. T. Armistead, was unable to sleep that night because of the ruckus. Jennie Simpson, a chambermaid at the hotel, also heard the fight. Mr. Monroe wanted to cash in some of his wife's jewelry for gambling money. She kept refusing, and he kept giving her whiskey.

The next morning, Sunday, January 21, around nine or ten o'clock, the two appeared at breakfast at a local restaurant, their differences apparently reconciled. One man, Frank Malloy, stated that he saw Bessie at the table wearing large diamond rings. That afternoon the couple strolled cheerfully across the bridge over Big Cypress Creek, the man carrying a picnic basket containing two bottles of beer, chicken sandwiches, and assorted condiments that he had ordered at a local restaurant.

Mr. Monroe returned later that afternoon by himself. When asked about his wife, he replied that she was visiting friends and would meet him later. He added that they planned to leave town on the Tuesday morning train. On Tuesday, January 23, the cleaning crew at the hotel found the Monroes' room empty. Some people had observed Mr. Monroe early that morning, carrying all the baggage he and his wife had brought with them, boarding the eastbound train. Bessie was not in sight.

A. Monroe was the assumed name of Abraham Rothschild. Abe was born in Cincinnati, Ohio, in 1853, the son of Meyer (or Meier) Rothschild, an affluent dealer in precious stones, and Abe began working in the family business at a young age. As he matured he was described as tall, handsome, and an advocate of the "good life." A sound businessman with a glorious future, his propensity for wine and women often led him astray.

In an effort to get his son away from the temptations of the big city, Abe's father handed him a sample case of jewelry and sent him on the road as a traveling salesman. If the elder Rothschild had hoped such a maneuver would serve to keep Abe on the straight and narrow, he was sadly mistaken. Not only did traveling broaden the young man's appetites, it brought him in contact with a woman who would change his life.

Bessie Moore was born Annie Stone in 1854 in Syracuse, New York. Her father was a successful shoe merchant, and from all indications Annie was comfortable and well educated. Despite this, she took up with a man named Moore when she was fifteen years old. Though the two never married during their brief association, Annie retained Moore as her last name. Some believe she became a prostitute after the relationship ended, and somewhere down the line she changed Annie to Bessie.

It is reputed that Bessie inherited a large sum of money upon her father's death. A beautiful woman with creamy white skin, black hair, sparkling gray eyes, and an admirable figure, she added to her monetary assets with expensive jewelry lavished on her by her many male admirers. She practiced the oldest profession first in Cincinnati and later in New Orleans and Hot Springs, Arkansas. While in Cincinnati Bessie reportedly worked in the Mansion of Joy on Broadway. A magnetic woman of good breeding and intelligence, Bessie was the center of male attention.

It was in Hot Springs that the star-crossed lovers first met. Bessie's beauty and charm immediately caught Abe's eye, while Abe's good looks, coupled with his occupation as a jewelry salesman, made the attraction mutual. The two were well suited for each other and inseparable from the start.

From what little is known, it seems Abe mesmerized the lovely young woman and kept her under his thumb. Records reveal that he beat her on several occasions and

Abe Rothschild and "Diamond Bessie" Moore, from a Dallas Morning News *article.* —Courtesy Texas/Dallas History and Archives Division, Dallas Public Library

took money from her. Around Christmas in 1875, in Cincinnati, they both appeared in public drunk and Abe hit Bessie so hard he knocked her down. The next year, Abe pressed her into prostitution and demanded that she give him fifty dollars a day from her earnings. When she refused, Abe beat her so brutally he was thrown into jail. In time, Bessie became a heavy drinker and addicted to stimulants.

In spite of the way Abe treated her, Bessie traveled with him as his wife. There is no record the two ever married, though some contend they met in Cincinnati and were wed in Danville, Indiana, on their way to Arkansas. Others allege a ceremony took place in the little town of Linden, Texas, fifteen miles north of Jefferson. Even if never made legal, their union could be considered a common-law marriage.

Why would Abe want to rid himself of a woman as beautiful and devoted as Bessie? There is speculation that somehow she had become an albatross around his neck. She may have been trying to push Abe to the altar, threatening to approach Abe's father about their affair if he refused to marry her, perhaps because she was pregnant. Although the autopsy did not confirm a pregnancy, several witnesses testified that Bessie appeared to be expecting when they saw her on the streets of Jefferson shortly before her death.

In December 1876 Bessie and Abe took a riverboat from Cincinnati to New Orleans, arriving a few days after the New Year's celebration. Bessie purchased some new luggage there, which she had personalized, "Annie

Moore, New Orleans." From Louisiana the couple traveled by train to Texas. They reached Marshall and registered at the Capitol Hotel on January 17, 1877, two days before arriving in Jefferson. Within a week, Bessie would be dead.

The day after Abe Rothschild left Jefferson, a heavy snow, coupled with cold winds, blanketed the town. After the weather cleared two weeks later, Sarah King, a local woman who lived less than a mile south of Jefferson on the Marshall Road, was gathering firewood just south of Big Cypress Creek Bridge in the late afternoon of February 5. What she saw made her forget her task and run to town. There she reported to a man named Sims that she had found a woman's body; Sims, in turn, notified Justice of the Peace C. C. Beckford.

Beckford and Constable A. J. Stambaugh hastened to the site. The corpse was positioned about a foot from a pine log, the victim of a gunshot to the head. Stambaugh surveyed evidence of a picnic near the body: brown wrapping paper with bread crumbs, a nearly empty beer bottle, chicken bones, and fragments of pickles. The body was not disheveled; in fact, the woman's stylish and expensive clothing was not mussed at all. She lay on her back, her left arm across her stomach. Bugs covered her face, eyes, and nose. The lawmen found no jewelry on the body.

The constable stated that he had seen the victim on the street two weeks earlier. Justice Beckford immediately set an inquest in motion. Unable to complete their task before dark, Beckford and Stambaugh secured a carriage and moved the corpse to the coroner's office in Jefferson. They questioned Brooks House employees about the woman. Beckford directed local women Isabella Gouldy, Mollie Turk, and four others to disrobe the body, inventory all items found on her person, and prepare the corpse for burial.

Once the news of the murder became public knowledge, the townspeople collected $150 to cover burial expenses. The dead woman was laid to rest in Oakwood Cemetery in Jefferson. The grave was left unmarked because no one was certain of her name.

The body was eventually identified as that of Bessie Moore. On February 18, Justice Beckford issued a warrant for the arrest of A. Monroe on suspicion of murder, since, as far as they knew, he was the last person to see the victim alive. The following day, after Constable Stambaugh reported that there was no one in Marion County named A. Monroe, the lawmen received a lead. C. H. Pepper, owner of Capitol Hotel in Marshall, twenty-five miles south of Jefferson, recognized the description of Monroe and Moore as a couple who had registered at his hotel as "A. Rothschild and wife, Cincinnati, Ohio." With Pepper's information, further verified by railroad officials, Beckford issued a new warrant for the arrest of A. Rothschild, which he telegraphed to law officials in Cincinnati.

While the authorities gathered information in Jefferson, Abe Rothschild was back in Cincinnati, after brief sojourns in Memphis and New York. Perhaps due to a guilty conscience, Abe had become paranoid, swearing someone was following him. One night, after a particularly heavy bout with John Barleycorn, he walked from the pub to a large, open yard across the street. There he put a pistol to his head and attempted suicide. All he managed to accomplish, however, was the loss of his right eye.

While he was in the hospital being treated for his wound, Abe was served the warrant from Texas and local police immediately arrested him. When he refused to return to Texas to face charges, Beckford appealed to Texas Governor Richard B. Hubbard for a warrant of extradition, which was approved in short order. Hubbard appointed John M. Vines, former sheriff of Marion County, to escort the prisoner back to Jefferson for trial.

Although Abe was now even more of a black sheep than before, his family gathered around him in support. They hired a lawyer, who filed a writ of habeas corpus to circumvent the extradition. The court denied the writ on March 19, but it did grant a delay of twenty days to allow the accused time to recuperate from his wound. When the stay was up, Vines and a deputy escorted their prisoner to Jefferson, arriving on April 11, 1877, whereupon they placed Abe in the county lockup.

The Texas governor sent letters to a private firm requesting assistance in the prosecution, but it was two Texas assistant attorneys general who signed on to the case. For the defense, the wealthy Rothschilds hired the best, including Charles A. Culberson, future governor of Texas; his father, David B. Culberson, a United States senator; and William Armistead, the elder Culberson's law partner. The high-profile case offered much prestige for lawyers on both sides as well as a great deal of cash for the defense team. Armistead reportedly stated that the fee he and the other defense lawyers received was "sufficient to retain them for the remainder of their lives." No dollar figure was ever released, but rumors abounded that they were paid with kegs of gold and silver.

Abe's parents came to Jefferson for their son's trial. The grand jury rendered an indictment for murder on April 26, assigning a trial date of May 9. On May 4 prosecuting attorney Edward Guthridge filed a motion to quash the indictment because the Bill of Indictment was "defective" and wouldn't secure a conviction in court. The indictment was dismissed. The second indictment was filed the same day, and the trial was set for May 24.

The defense then filed for a continuance in the absence of witnesses Clara Ames and Mollie Shannon. They claimed that both women stated that the body in the photographs was not Bessie Moore but one Alice Kirby, who had been in Jefferson in early February 1877. This part of the motion was invalidated when Kirby family members, upon examining the photograph, admitted that there was a resemblance but that it was not Alice Kirby. The picture in question was eventually verified to be of Bessie Moore.

The motion of continuance also charged outside influence by the state. The governor's attorneys, the motion alleged, attempted to secure witnesses of questionable character and benefit. The continuance was granted and the case delayed a full year.

On August 1, 1877, the defense filed an application for a writ of habeas corpus, primarily to have bail established for their client. Judge B. T. Estes denied the writ and set a new trial date of November 1877. An appeal of the ruling to the Texas Court of Appeals was denied. In the meantime, the trial was moved back again to May 1878.

Shortly before the trial date, the defense filed several other motions, the most prominent claiming that the county attorney Edward Guthridge was present when the grand jury voted on the indictment. Judge Estes overruled the motion. The defense then requested a change of venue, arguing that their client could not receive a fair hearing in Jefferson. The judge granted the request and the proceedings were moved a short distance south, to Marshall, and assigned to District Judge A. J. Booty's court. The trial was delayed further when lawyers on both sides claimed pressing business elsewhere.

Once under way, the trial lasted three weeks (most of December 1878); the closing arguments took three days. The jury found Abe Rothschild guilty of murder in the first degree and sentenced him to the gallows. Adding insult to injury, the condemned man was assessed costs for the trial and for the hanging.

Yet the saga was far from over. The defense appealed the sentence to Judge George Clark of the Seventh Texas Court of Appeals, claiming unfairness. They said the court had ignored the defense's protest over the selection of one of the jurors, William Sanders. Sanders had stated unequivocally that he had an opinion on the case and in essence would not change his opinion regardless of the evidence presented. Judge Clark agreed that the court had been remiss and stated that Sanders "was not a fit person to pass upon the life of the prisoner." In addition, the judge ruled on the defense's reiteration of the earlier charge that County Attorney Guthridge was present when the grand jury voted on the indictment. Clark's final ruling: a mistrial. Furthermore, on November 24, 1880, the District Court of Harrison County voided Abe Rothschild's original indictment.

The Rothschild case received a lot of publicity across the state, and most editorials thought the guilty verdict was just. When Judge Clark reversed the decision—regardless of his legal reasoning—he suffered every indignity except tar and feathering. At the next state convention, he wasn't even renominated for the bench.

Not to be outmaneuvered, the prosecution reindicted Abe Rothschild on December 2, 1880; the second trial began in Jefferson twelve days later. Judge Estes, fed up with the Rothschild case by this time, was determined that these proceedings would be the last. Jury selection began on December 16 and ended by December 22; the trial got under way that same afternoon. News coverage of the event brought so many onlookers, they overflowed into the street. Judge Estes ordered additional law enforcement to protect Rothschild against potential mob violence.

The defense's case revolved around the testimony of Isabella (Belle) Gouldy. Gouldy had been one of the matrons assigned to prepare Bessie Moore's body for burial. She testified that she had seen Moore with a man on January 20 and January 25. The man, she stated emphatically, was not the defendant, Abraham Rothschild. If this was true, then Diamond Bessie was still alive two days after Abe boarded the eastbound train.

The prosecution sought to discredit Gouldy's testimony. The attorney asserted that the witness had once been employed by the Greenlight in Marshall, a place of questionable reputation. Gouldy denied the allegation. She was further accused of abandoning her parents and younger siblings. She admitted that this was true but stated that she had returned home upon hearing of her mother's terminal illness two years before, and that she had been caring for her father and siblings ever since.

Another black mark on Gouldy's character was the fact that she had been sharing quarters with Mollie and Dave Turk, a couple "cohabiting in sin." She swore she had no knowledge that they were unmarried. Gouldy also invoked the fifth Amendment several times during her testimony, further eroding her credibility. Yet the defense witness did succeed in planting seeds of doubt in the minds of the jurors.

The defense lawyers also stressed the condition of the dead body. From the time Bessie was first noticed missing until Sarah King found her, fifteen days had elapsed. A body could not be so well preserved after such a length of time; therefore, the murder must have taken place after their client had left Jefferson. The prosecution rebounded with the argument that the cold weather at the time Bessie was slain could account for preservation of the body. The spot where she was found was "scarcely reached by sunlight for two hours in any day of the year," they said.

The Marion County ex officio coroner, Dr. Turner, challenged the prosecution's declaration. He believed that despite the weather, the body was too well preserved to have been exposed to the elements for two weeks. Furthermore, he continued, the scraps of food still on the ground would have been eaten by animals within that time.

The defense followed with an accusation that some chicanery took place while their client was incarcerated in Harrison County. A horse thief named Quincy Harmon was put in the cell with Rothschild, and the two were caught trying to saw their way out of jail. The defense asserted that Harmon was a "ringer," placed in the cell to dig the hole of Rothschild's guilt a little deeper, giving the prosecution a stronger case for indicting the defendant.

As evidence of more government tampering, the defense presented a letter by Governor Hubbard, stressing his willingness to put the power of the state, via the attorney general, in the thick of things if need be. This was an intrusion into local affairs by the state.

One participant in the trial who became something of a star was the prosecution's main witness, Jennie Simpson, the chambermaid at Brooks House. Imbued with her own celebrity, Simpson gave a flamboyant performance, and on several occasions the bench reprimanded her to stop expounding on her answers. She offered emotional diatribes about the anguish she witnessed Bessie Moore suffer at Abe Rothschild's hands. She also testified that she saw Rothschild at breakfast the morning after Moore's disappearance wearing the rings the victim had worn the day before.

To cross-examine Simpson, the defense chose David Culberson, whose skillful tactics may well have been the key factor in turning the jurors' opinions in Rothschild's favor. Culberson challenged virtually every word of Simpson's testimony. The witness became flustered and started backpedaling on her statements. She finally erupted in anger. In the end, Culberson's cross-examination effectively nullified Simpson's entire testimony.

Closing arguments concluded around four in the afternoon of December 30, 1880. Four hours later the jury returned a verdict of not guilty. Abe Rothschild stood, smiled, and shook the hands of his attorneys. Judge Estes ordered everyone in the courtroom to remain seated except the defendant and his parents, who were escorted from the room by the sheriff and his deputies. The Rothschilds boarded the next train east.

Thus ended one of the most famous trials in Texas history. Officials in Marion County never accepted the verdict. Nevertheless, they marked the case "unsolved," and it remains so to this day.

Rumors, bound to pop up in cases such as this, began to circulate immediately after the trial and continued for years. It was said that the verdict was revealed just as a train, sitting at the station, blew its whistle. At that instant, Abe and his parents ran out of the courthouse and jumped into a waiting carriage, which whisked them to the depot. They scurried onto the train and were never heard from again.

Other rumors insinuated shady dealings with the jury. One claimed that while the jury was in deliberation, twelve $1,000 bills were lowered through a trap door in the ceiling. Another whisper had it that each of the jurors took piano lessons on instruments given to them soon after the trial. There was also a story that all twelve jurors met untimely deaths within a year of the trial.

Abe Rothschild, it was buzzed, was later imprisoned for twenty years for grand theft. Others said that the rigors of the trial and the guilt over his past drained him so much that he took off for Europe, where he lived the rest of his life.

One intriguing story emerged about a decade after the trial. In the 1890s a mysterious figure stepped down from the train in Jefferson and inquired about the grave of a woman named Bessie Moore. At the cemetery he knelt in prayer and placed some roses on the grave. The man thanked the custodian, F. B. Schweers, for taking such good care of the site and handed him a ten-dollar bill. The stranger then boarded a train and left Jefferson forever.

Was this man Abe Rothschild? No one knows. He was described as tall and handsome, with an aged face.

In addition, he wore a patch over his right eye—the same eye Abe had shot out in his suicide attempt.

In the 1930s, some fifty years after the murder and burial of Bessie Moore, there appeared a stone marker over her grave. The stone showed her name engraved inside a diamond-shaped frame. No one knew who ordered it, or who put it in place. It wasn't until April 1941 that local foundry operator E. B. McDonald admitted erecting the stone. He and his son carved it and drove to Oakwood Cemetery in the middle of the night to set it in place. He did it, he said, because "it had not seemed right for Diamond Bessie to sleep in an unmarked grave." Today the gravesite is surrounded by a

Diamond Bessie's gravesite —Author photo

metal fence with a sign attached. On the stone, time has virtually eradicated the McDonalds' engraving.

In 1955 citizens of Jefferson began an annual ritual, the Murder Trial of Diamond Bessie, played out over three days in late April. Locals perform all the roles, with actual judges and attorneys playing those parts. While the reenactment is based on the transcript of the trial, cast members often ad lib many of their lines. The show is well attended and serves to preserve old stories and generate new theories. So the mystery of Diamond Bessie lingers on.

Sites of Interest

The Alamo in San Antonio is Texas's most visited tourist attraction, and rightly so. While the first shot of the Texas Revolution was fired a few miles south in Gonzales, the Alamo personifies the extent to which people will go to gain independence. While the site today is only a fraction of the original size of the old mission and is set down in the middle of a bustling city of more than a million people, it is nevertheless a must-see for history buffs.

Less than one hundred miles south of San Antonio is another site worth visiting. In the small town of Goliad is the Presidio La Bahía. Not only is this the best-preserved Spanish fort west of the Mississippi River, it is also site of the Goliad Massacre of March 1836. Within easy walking distance is the Fannin Monument, site of the largest mass grave on American soil, with some three hundred bodies interred there.

The Presidio La Bahia, sitting on a lonely, virtually isolated plain, still appears as a viewer would expect it to have looked like in the early nineteenth century. It still has the room where almost 350 men were imprisoned, such small quarters that there was no room to lie down. The parade ground, where Francisca Alavez convinced the presidio commander to allow the prisoners to move, is still intact. The small church, still in use, has also withstood the ravages of time.

Excellent general sources for Texas history are:

Center for American History
Sid Richardson Hall 2.101
University of Texas at Austin
Austin, TX 78712
512-495-4515
www.cah.texas.edu

Daughters of the Republic of Texas Library
P.O. Box 1401
Alamo Plaza
San Antonio, TX 78295-1401
210-225-1071 or 210-225-8155
www.drtl.org/index.html

Handbook of Texas Online
www.tsha.utexas.edu/handbook/online

Texas State Library and Archives
1201 Brazos Austin, TX 78701
512-463-5455
www.tsl.state.tx.us

INDIVIDUAL SITES OF INTEREST:

Susanna Dickinson
Austin City Library History Center
810 Guadalupe Street
Austin, TX 78701
512-499-7480
www.ci.austin.tx.us/library/ibahc.htm

Dr. Eugene Clark Library
901 Bois d'Arc Avenue
Lockhart, TX 78644
512-398-3223

Francisca Alavez
Fannin Battleground State Historical Park
Contact: Park Superintendent
Goliad State Historical Park
P.O. Box 727
Goliad, TX 77963
512-645-3405
www.tpwd.state.tx.us/park/fannin

Presidio La Bahia
Box 57
Goliad, TX 77963
512-645-3752
www.iitexas.com/gpages/goliad.htm

Emily Morgan
San Jacinto Battleground State Historical Park
San Jacinto Museum of History
3800 Park Road 1836
La Porte, TX 77571
713-479-2421
www.tpwd.state.tx.us/park/battlesh

Lottie Deno
Fort Griffin State Historical Park
Route 1, Box 125
Albany, TX 76430
915-762-3592
www.tpwd.state.tx.us/park/fortgrif

Frontier Times Museum
Bandera, TX 78003
830-796-3864

Marshall Memorial Library
301 South Tin
Deming, NM 88030

Pamelia Mann
Houston Public Library
Houston Metropolitan Research Center
500 McKinney Street
Houston, TX 77002
713-247-1661
www.hpl.lib.tx.us/hpl/hmrc.html

Sally Scull
French G. Simpson Memorial Library
P.O. Drawer 269
Hallettsville, TX 77964-0269
361-798-3243

Nesbitt Memorial Library
529 Washington Street
Columbus, TX 78934-2326
979-732-3392

Sarah Hornsby
Bastrop County Historical Museum
702 Main Street
Bastrop, TX 78602
512-303-0057
www.hornsbybend.com

Diamond Bessie
Jefferson Historical Society Museum
223 West Austin Street
Jefferson, TX 75657
903-665-2775

Sources

General

In researching this book I have used innumerable sources from the archives and resource centers at the Center for American History, University of Texas, Austin; the Daughters of the Republic of Texas Library, the Alamo, San Antonio; and the Texas State Library and Archives, Austin.

When I begin a project about Texas history, I turn first to T. R. Fehrenbach's *Lone Star: A History of Texas and the Texans* (New York: Collier Books, 1968). It is the book upon which the PBS series of the same name was based. I will soon have to buy another copy; my current one is getting quite tattered.

Another main source, not necessarily second, is the excellent six-volume series, *The New Handbook of Texas*, Ron Tyler, ed. (Austin: Texas State Historical Association, 1996). Each volume is about a thousand pages long, and the supplement, released in 2000, is almost two thousand pages. Virtually anything to do with Texas history, from early Indian occupation to the present day, can be found in either this work or in Fehrenbach's.

A third useful general source is *The Portable Handbook of Texas*, Roy R. Barley and Mark F. Odintz, eds.

(Austin: Texas State Historical Association, 2000). The following are sources specific to each chapter.

1. Susanna Dickinson: Alamo Survivor

Abbott, Carroll. "Little Angel Who Fell." *Sir*, January 1956, 40.

"Adjutant General's Letters concerning the Alamo, 1875–1878." Texas State Archives, Austin.

Application for Bounty and Donation Lands (witnessed by mark of Susannah Dickinson), 8 March 1860. Daughters of the Republic of Texas Library, the Alamo, San Antonio.

Bateman, Audray. "Hannig History." *Austin American-Statesman*, 13 April 1984.

Benefiel, B. J. "Alamo Remembered." *Lockhart Post-Register*, 6 March 1986.

Bishop, Curt. "Alamo Heroine Found Happiness in Austin." *Austin Times Herald*, 7 September 1961.

Brogan, Evelyn. *James Bowie: A Hero of the Alamo.* San Antonio: Theodore Kunzman, Publisher, 1922.

Callihan, Elmer L. "Later Romantic Years of Mrs. Dickinson." *Dallas Morning News*, 9 March 1930.

Carroll, Bess. "Santa Anna Admits Defeat." *San Antonio Light*, 8 March 1936.

_____. "Survivor Tells of Fall." *San Antonio Light*, 18 March 1936.

Davis, Joe Tom. *Legendary Texians*. Vol. 2. Austin: Eakin Press, 1985.

Eastin, Ben C. "An Austin Newspaper in 1849." *Dallas Morning News*, 15 May 1927.

Farber, James. "Bride of the Alamo." *American Weekly*, 1 March 1953, 12.

Garcia, James E. "A Traitor by Any Other Name." *Austin American-Statesman*, 6 September 1991.

Green, Rena Maverick, ed. *Memoirs of Mary A. Maverick and Her Son Geo. Madison Maverick*. San Antonio: Alamo Printing, 1921.

Halpenny, Marie. "Lady of the Alamo." *Texas Parade*, January 1956, 31.

King, C. Richard. *Susanna Dickinson: Messenger of the Alamo*. Austin: Shoal Creek Publishers, 1976.

Kingston, Mike, ed. "Texas History." *1986–1987 Texas Almanac*. Dallas: Dallas Morning News, 1985.

Malec, Walter. ". . . At Daniels on the Lavaca." *Lavaca County Tribune*, n.d.

Marks, Paula Mitchell. "The Men of Gonzales: They Answered the Call." *American History Illustrated*, March 1986, 46.

Masur, E. A., to L. W. Kemp, 24 August 1939, and E. A. Masur to Boyce House, 26 September 1845. Photocopies. Daughters of the Republic of Texas Library, the Alamo, San Antonio.

McCallum, Jane Y. "The Alamo Had One." (Source and date of article unknown.) Daughters of the Republic of Texas Library, the Alamo, San Antonio.

"Memorial to Honor Historical Marker." *Austin American-Statesman*, 1 March 1976.

Mims, Evelyn Hornsby. "Messenger of Defeat." *Nashville Tennessean Magazine,* 27 November 1955.

Morphis, J. M. *History of Texas.* New York: U.S. Publishing, 1875.

Nitschke, Mrs. Willard Griffith. "A Nation Is Born." *Texas Parent-Teacher*, March 1949, 7.

Oldenburg, Helen. "Woman Survivor of Alamo Lived a Most Exciting Life." *Austin American-Statesman*, 6 March 1969.

Shenkman, Richard, and Kurt Reiger. *One-night Stands with American History.* New York: Quill, 1982.

Shuffler, R. Henderson. "The Heroine of the Alamo." *Houston Chronicle-Texas Magazine*, 29 November 1964.

Sinclair, Dorothy Tutt. *Tales of the Texians.* Bellaire, Tex.: Dorothy Sinclair Enterprises, 1985.

Spencer, Gayle. "Susanna Dickinson Survived the Battle of the Alamo." *Paseo del Rio Showboat*, June 1978.

"Survived Alamo Massacre; Her First Picture in Print." *San Antonio Express*, 24 February 1929.

Texas State Legislature. Speech on Joint Resolution for Relief of Infant Daughter of Susannah and Almeron Dickinson. Guy M. Bryan. 1850. Daughters of the Republic of Texas Library, the Alamo, San Antonio.

Tolbert, Frank X. "Finding Susanna's Grave at Sun Up." *Dallas Morning News*, 28 February 1961.

Ward, Ray. "Ring Coming Back to Alamo Home." *San Antonio Light*, 13 May 1955.

Webb, Walter Prescott, ed. *The Handbook of Texas.* Vol. 2. Austin: Texas State Historical Association, 1952.

2. Francisca Alavez: The Angel of Goliad

Couch, Ernie and Jill, comps. *Texas Trivia*. Nashville: Rutledge Press, 1991.

Davenport, Harbert. "The Men of Goliad." *Southwestern Historical Quarterly* 48 (July 1939): 1–27.

Edwards, Janet R. "Remembering Goliad." *Texas Parks & Wildlife*, November 1992, 18.

Goliad Texas Express, 22 January 1987.

Grasslhof, Ray. "Town with a Mission." *Austin American-Statesman*, 27 March 1993.

Hamilton, Lester. *Goliad Survivor: Isaac D. Hamilton.* San Antonio: Naylor Co., 1971.

Huson, Hobart. *Refugio 1*. Woodson, Tex.: Brooke Foundation, 1953.

Knaggs, John. "Tragic Event in Texas History Recalled." *Austin American-Statesman*, 3 April 1993.

LaRoche, Clarence J. "The Angel of Goliad." *San Antonio Express News*, 1 August 1954.

"Remember Goliad? Along with the Alamo, See Presidio La Bahia." *Austin American-Statesman*, 18 October 1992.

Ruff, Ann. "Angel of Goliad." *Texas Highways*, August 1986, 18.

Selden, Jack. "Remember Goliad!" *Texas Highways*, October 1984, 24.

Smith, Ruby Cumby. "James W. Fannin, Jr., in the Texas Revolution." *Southwestern Historical Quarterly* 23 (October 1919): 79–90, 171–203, 271–283.

Teer, L. P. "Angel of Goliad." *The West*, July 1965, 19.

Tolbert, Frank X. "Tolbert's Texas." *Dallas News*, 8 February 1956.

Walraven, Bill. "Angel of Goliad Aided Many Texians." *Goliad Advance Guard*, 22 March 1990.

———. "Not All Has Been Told about the Angel of Goliad." *Corpus Christi Caller Times*, 10 October 1986.

Webb, Walter Prescott, ed. *The Handbook of Texas*. Vol. 2. Austin: Texas State Historical Association, 1952.

Wortham, Louis J. *A History of Texas*. Vol. 3. Fort Worth: Wortham-Molyneaux Co., 1924.

Young, Richard Alan, and John Dockery, eds. *Ghost Stories from the American Southwest*. Little Rock: August House Publishers, 1991.

3. Emily Morgan: The Yellow Rose of Texas

Abernethy, Francis Edward, ed. *Legendary Ladies of Texas*. Denton: University of North Texas Press, 1994.

Davis, Joe Tom. *Legendary Texians*. Vol. 3. Austin: Eakin Press, 1986.

Fluent, Michael. "San Jacinto." *American History Illustrated*, May 1986, 22.

Moss, Sue Winton. "The Battle That Shaped a Nation." *Texas Parks & Wildlife*, April 1992, 5.

Nevin, David. "'Fight and Be Damned!'" Said Sam Houston." *Smithsonian*, July 1992, 82.

"The Original Yellow Rose of Texas." *Strange Stories: Amazing Facts of America's Past.* Pleasantville, N.Y.: Reader's Digest, 1989.

Rambie, Fount, and Ann Galloway. "Speaking of Texas." *Texas Highways*, April 1995, 3.

Shenkman, Richard, and Kurt Reiger. *One-night Stands with American History.* New York: Quill, 1982.

Webb, Walter Prescott, ed. *The Handbook of Texas.* Vol. 2. Austin: Texas State Historical Association, 1952.

4. Lottie Deno: She "Dealt" with the Best of Them

Beesley, Frank. "Outpost on the Clear Fork." *Texas Highways*, October 1983, 10.

Biggers, Don. *Shackelford County Sketches.* Ed. Joan Farmer. Albany, Tex.: Clear Fork Press, 1974.

Blakely, Mike. "Doc Holliday Eludes Noose." *Austin American-Statesman*, 12 August 1985.

Brown, Dee. "The Day of the Buffalo." *American History Illustrated*, July 1976, 4.

Cashion, Ty. "(Gun)Smoke Gets in Your Eyes: A Revisionist Look at 'Violent' Fort Griffin." *Southwestern Historical Quarterly* 99 (July 1995): 80–94.

Clarke, Ollie E., comp. *Fort Griffin.* Brochure. Albany (Texas) Chamber of Commerce, September 1935.

Cox, Mike. Review of *The Frontier World of Fort Griffin: The Life and Death of a Western Town*, by Charles Robinson III. *Austin American-Statesman*, 6 September 1992.

Flores, Dan. "The Long Shadow of the Buffalo." *Texas Parks & Wildlife*, June 1992, 7.

Gard, Wayne. *The Chisholm Trail*. Norman: University of Oklahoma Press, 1954.

_____. *Rawhide Texas*. Norman: University of Oklahoma Press, 1965.

Holden, Frances Mayhugh. *Lambshead Before Interwoven*. College Station: Texas A & M University Press, 1982.

Hunter, J. Marvin. *The Story of Lottie Deno: Her Life and Times*. Bandera, Tex.: Four Hunters, 1959.

McIlvain, Myra Hargrave. "Outpost on the Clear Fork." *Texas Highways*, May 1991, 50.

Matthews, Sallie Reynolds. *Interwoven: A Pioneer Chronicle*. College Station: Texas A & M University Press, 1982.

Nordyce, Lewis. Great *Roundup: The Story of Texas and Southwestern Cowmen*. New York: William Morrow, 1955.

Richardson, Rupert N. *Along Texas Old Forts Trail*. Abilene, Tex.: Neil Fry, 1972.

Rister, Carl Coke. *Fort Griffin on the Texas Frontier*. Norman: University of Oklahoma Press, 1956.

Robinson, Charles M., III. *Frontier Forts of Texas*. Houston: Lone Star Books, 1986.

Rose, Cynthia. *Lottie Deno: Gambling Queen of Hearts*. Santa Fe: Clear Light Publishers, 1994.

Rye, Edgar. *The Quirt and the Spur*. Austin: Steck-Vaughn Co., 1967.

Webb, Walter Prescott, ed. *The Handbook of Texas*. Vol. 2. Austin: Texas State Historical Association, 1952.

White, Ann P. "Guardian of the Clear Fork Country." *Texas Parks & Wildlife*, September 1994, 18.

Wiltsey, Norman B. "World's Greatest Slaughter." *Old West*, Fall 1966, 16.

Woolford, Sam. "Lady Gambler 'Angel of San Antonio.'" *San Antonio Light*, 27 September 1959.

_____. "Posthumous Book Solves Enigma of Angel of S.A." *San Antonio Light*, 20 September 1959.

5. Pamelia Mann: As Mean as They Come

Boatright, Mody C., ed. *Mexican Border Ballads and Other Lore*. Austin: Texas Folklore Society, 1946.

Davis, Joe Tom. *Legendary Texians*. Vol. 2. Austin: Eakin Press, 1985.

Haley, James L. *Texas: An Album of History*. New York: Doubleday, 1985.

Harrison, Fred. "Pamelia Mann: Texas Tigress." *The West*, August 1965, 40.

Hogan, William Ransom. "Pamelia Mann: Texas Frontierswoman." *Southwest Review* 20, October 1934–July 1935, 360–370.

Myers, Cindi. "Speaking of Texas." *Texas Highways*, December 1991, 3.

"Queen of Vice Rules over Texas Empire." *News–San Antonio*, 5 November 1979.

Turner, Martha Anne. *Sam Houston and His Twelve Women.* Austin: Pemberton Press, 1966.

Webb, Walter Prescott, ed. *The Handbook of Texas.* Vol. 2. Austin: Texas State Historical Association, 1952.

6. Sally Scull: Woe to Those Who Crossed Her

Abernethy, Francis Edward, ed. *Legendary Ladies of Texas.* Denton: University of North Texas Press, 1994.

Boethel, Paul C. *Colonel Amasa Turner, the Gentleman from Lavaca, and Other Captains at San Jacinto.* Austin: Von Boeckman-Jones, 1963.

Hill, Luther H. "The Tragic Story of Sally Scull." Speech delivered at annual dinner meeting of the San Antonio Historical Association, San Antonio, 18 January 1974. Photocopy from Daughters of the Republic of Texas Library, the Alamo, San Antonio.

Hunter, John Warren. *Heel-fly Time in Texas.* Bandera, Tex.: Frontier Times, 1931.

Huson, Hobart. *Refugio 2.* Woodsboro, Tex.: Brooke Foundation, 1955.

Malec, Walter. "More to It than a Mere Name." *Lavaca County Tribune*, 22 June 1962.

Myers, Cindi. "Speaking of Texas." *Texas Highways*, November 1992, 3.

Nolan, Oran Warder. "Banquete's Gun-toting Woman Horse Trader, Sally Skull, Was Never an Outlaw: She

Could Ride, Shoot and Curse, and Had Many Friends." *Corpus Christi Caller*, 4 March 1937.

Woods, Dee. "Sally Skulle, Horse Trader with a Six Gun." *The West*, April 1965, 40.

7. Sarah Hornsby: Prophet or Dreamer?

Auer, Louise Cheney. "Miracle of Josiah Wilbarger." *Real West*, September 1965, 51.

Bagby, Nathe P. "'Quiet,' Said the Ghost, 'Help Is Near.'" *Dallas Morning News*, 12 June 1927.

Dobie, J. Frank. *I'll Tell You a Tale*. Austin: University of Texas Press, 1931.

Hart, Weldon. "Cen-Tex Pioneer Lived to Tell of Being Scalped." *Austin American-Statesman*, 6 June 1937.

Herndon, John. "The Legend of Josiah Wilbarger." *Austin American-Statesman*, 18 June 1985.

Kelley, Mike. "Dream Power Lifts Josiah Wilbarger's Story into Local Lore." *Austin American-Statesman*, 9 September 1987.

Rucker, Ellie. Column on location of Wilbarger marker. *Austin American-Statesman*, 25 September 1985.

Wilbarger, J. S. *Indian Depredations in Texas*. Austin: The Pemberton Press, 1967.

8. Diamond Bessie: The Mystery Lingers

Hudson, Wilson M., ed. *Diamond Bessie and the Shepherds*. Austin: Encino Press, 1972.

Mallory, Randy. "Rooms with a Boo." *Texas Highways*, October 1997, 22.

Markchuk, Jim. "Stage Lights Shine on Old Crime." *Journal*. March–April 1997.

McCutchan, Ann. "Historic Port of Jefferson." *Austin American-Statesman*, 20 April 1997, 1.

"New Chapter Added to Hoary Bessie Death Mystery as Gravestone Donor Revealed." *Dallas Morning News*, 13 April 1941, 7.

Rodriguez, June Naylor. *Texas: Off the Beaten Path.* Old Saybrook, Conn.: Globe Pequot Press, 1994.

Russell, Traylor. *The Diamond Bessie Murder and the Rothschild Trials.* Reprint, Waco, Tex.: Texian Press, 1990.

Scales, Shirley, and Carolyn Ramsey. "Mystery and Murder of Diamond Bessie." *Dallas Morning News*, 8 January 1933, 1.

Syers, William E. *Backroads of Texas.* Houston: Gulf Publishing, 1993.

Walters, Mahlon L. "Who Done It? Rothschild in Retrospect." *Texas Bar Journal* 2 (February 1963): 108–166.

Index

About the Author

Don Blevins grew up in Johnson City, Tennessee, and at eighteen joined the Air Force, where he served for twenty-one years. In 1972 he retired to San Marcos, Texas, where he still lives. He earned his master of education degree from Southwest Texas State University in 1978, and he is currently a member of the Texas State Historical Association and the Austin Writers' League. Blevins has penned dozens of articles on history, travel, and other subjects. His first book, *Peculiar, Uncertain, and Two Egg*, was published in 2000 by Cumberland House.

Mr. Blevins is the father of three grown children, whose mother died in 1992. He gained another daughter, as well as three grandchildren, in 1994 when he married his current wife, Esther.

encourage you to patronize your local bookstore. Most stores will order any title they do
stock. You may also order directly from Mountain Press, using the order form provided
w or by calling our toll-free, 24-hour number and using your VISA, MasterCard,
cover or American Express.

es of interest:

__From Angels to Hellcats: Legendary Texas Women	paper/$12.00
__Chief Joseph and the Nez Perce: A Photographic History	paper/$15.00
__Crazy Horse: A Photographic Biography	paper/$20.00
__Lewis and Clark: A Photographic Journey	paper/$18.00
__The Oregon Trail: A Photographic Journey	paper/$18.00
__Photographing Montana, 1894–1928: The Life and Work of Evelyn Cameron	cloth/$35.00 paper/$16.00
__Roadside History of Texas	paper/$18.00
__Stories of Young Pioneers: In Their Own Words	paper/$14.00
__Women and Warriors of the Plains: The Pioneering Photograpy of Julia E. Tuell	paper/$18.00

Please include $3.00 per order to cover shipping and handling.

l the books marked above. I enclose $_____

ne _____

ress _____

/State/Zip _____

ayment enclosed (check or money order in U.S. funds)

ny: ☐VISA ☐MasterCard ☐Discover ☐American Express

l No. _____

ration Date: _____

ature _____

MOUNTAIN PRESS PUBLISHING COMPANY
P. O. Box 2399 • Missoula, MT 59806 • Fax 406-728-1635
Order Toll Free 1-800-234-5308 • Have your credit card ready
e-mail: mtnpress@montana.com • website: www.mountainpresspublish.com